Lovingly Dedicated To:

The ones who love the least of these … who love the child who seems unlikeable, difficult, alone, unwanted … "extra grace required."

For those of you who go that extra mile to not only tolerate each child, but you actively pursue each child for whom Christ died.

God bless your courage, your patience, and your faith in God's power to change a child's life forever. To all those in the trenches of children's ministry this weekend, we salute you.

YOUR CHILDREN'S MINISTRY BEYOND BASICS!

by Rev. Trisha R. Peach

TABLE OF CONTENTS

FORWARD

Standing in a walkway at a major children's ministry conference, I found myself smiling, laughing, nodding my head, and "amen-ing" the ministry insights that Trisha Peach was sharing with me. Fifteen minutes later, as she walked away, I thought, "No wonder this gal is so widely respected by her peers." Trisha brings passion, insight, and practical applicable advice to those who want to effectively reach and disciple kids today. By spending time absorbing the processes and recommendations Trisha gives, you will actually save yourself all kinds of time and pain. You'll be a step ahead of the problems, rather than trying to figure out how to solve the problems. Plant these "seeds" that Trisha shares in this book and you can have a ministry that bears much fruit. God bless and guide you in this exciting journey influencing the lives of these smaller saints.

Serving together,

Rev. Randy Christensen
Children's & Family Ministry Specialist qualityprograms.net

PREFACE

Welcome back friend! I truly expect great things for you and your kids' ministry in this exciting season. I have some questions for you. How are things going at your church right now? How are things in your children's ministry at this time? I know for many people numbers are a sensitive issue, and they certainly are NOT the whole story of the health of your ministry. If you're only talking numbers, that can be a warning sign that other very important aspects of ministry health, such as spiritual maturity, discipleship, and serving are being neglected. However, the hard truth is, numbers DO matter. Anything that is alive GROWS. If your ministry is not growing and not reaching new people then you are merely maintaining your social club as it slowly declines. On the flip side, if your church/ministry is growing and bringing in NEW people, you may, in fact, not realize how important and unusual that really is. The experts and researchers agree that "American Church attendance is steadily declining." Even more frightening, "Every year more than 4000 churches close their doors compared to just over 1000 new church starts! (Krejcir, 2006) These can be tough times to be in church leadership. And what that means is … if your ministry is reaching people and growing at all, you are in the minority. And that's the good news for you! Definitely worth celebrating! So what's the bad news? Think about this logically with me. Most of the 80 percent of churches we just talked about that are currently in decline used to be growing not that long ago. They used to be reaching new people, feeling the excitement of new adventures, bringing up new leaders and planning new building programs. Have you ever wondered, "What happened?" You should. It's a huge mistake (and a common one) to allow yourself to think, "All those other churches did everything wrong. We're special. We've found the formula. We're awesome. We will just keep busting out the doors forever!"

Not long ago, I went to Southern Illinois with my family. I will admit, when I heard "Southern Illinois" I was erroneously thinking, "Oh, near Chicago." But Southern Illinois, only 75 miles from Paducah, Kentucky, has its own very unique culture. Some of the distinctive features of this area are: friendly, loving people, good food, and … strangely enough … a whole bunch of empty, abandoned "mega" churches almost everywhere you look. I'm not kidding. It's creepy. I thought the locals were exaggerating. But I've seen at least five of them within a 9-mile radius—huge empty church buildings with neatly marked parking lots (now roped off). One of them had even purchased a Walmart; it was, in fact, one of the largest churches anywhere in the area. Now, it's an empty giant eyesore. And from what I heard, it all fizzled in such a SHORT time frame. What happened?

I cannot answer all the little details on the demise of each one of these churches or all the closed churches in your area, but I do know this. They didn't see it coming. They thought they had the formula all "figured out." Churches that die in a hurry usually have a catastrophic leadership failure—money or sex, etc. But, the majority of churches that die out, die a very slow death. And the reason? The very same wiz-bang that caused them to grow becomes their trap and their road to slow decline and then demise. How is that possible? Think about it. We like to find a routine, a plan, or a formula that works, and then do "that" over and over and over, always expecting the same results. I tell you what, my diet and workout routine that worked for me in college just doesn't work so well anymore. All those years and two kids later, it has had to adapt! Our culture changes, the country changes, the decade changes, but our churches stay stuck in what might have worked for them once upon a time.

Try this once just for kicks. Go into any church in America on a Sunday morning. Within a few moments, you can usually pick up on the decade, style, and strategy that first launched the church and got it to grow—60s, 80s? 90s? 2000? The problem is that we don't move past that church's first successes. The greatest threat for our church today is not the devil, or the world, or persecution. It's just us. We are the greatest threat—our complacency, ignorance, and internal arguing.

The enemy is REAL and he will use whatever he can to destroy a ministry that is thriving. So if your ministry is one of the rare ones that is actually growing, you had better be ready for a fight ... not against people, per se, but a fight more importantly than any of flesh and blood. We DON'T have time to rest on laurels. No Olympic runner sits down three-fourths of the way through the race and says, "Yeah, this is fine. I'll just stay here. This is good enough. "As a next generation leader, you will be called upon to go first. That will require courage. But in stepping out, you will give the gift of courage to those who are watching." (Andy Stanley)

If we're really looking for a formula, we would do well to remember this: Complacency + stagnation = death. Maintaining = slow decline. Think about the Dead Sea. It's called "dead" because it sits there, not moving, no inlets, and no outlets, just stagnant, calm waters. And the salt builds up day by day making sure nothing—NOTHING lives—hence, the name Dead Sea. And so it goes with the church. We need a steady stream of new ideas and fresh revelation (inlets) and new serving and giving opportunities (outlets) to keep going and growing. There must be constant evaluation, goal setting, and ongoing training. You will have to go back to the basics again and again, evaluating what your major challenges are NOW— recruiting, and training over and over again. There is no "floating." This river is moving fast. You are either fighting this culture upstream or sailing down with the rest. So refer back to that vision, your mission, and your base. You've got a great growing kids' ministry, so what now? Let's go forward. Ready?

"The most significant visions are not cast by great orators from a stage. They are cast at the bedsides of our children. The greatest vision casting opportunities happen between the hours of 7:30 and 9:30 PM Monday through Sunday. In these closing hours of the day we have a unique opportunity to plant the seeds of what could be and what should be. Take every opportunity you get." - Andy Stanley

CHAPTER ONE: TRANSITIONS

Is it normal to be switching staff every other year?

...or month?

"Joshua, you already know that Pastor Alan has let us know that he is leaving his position as children's pastor here at Zion Church. After such an amazing season of growth over these last 5 years, I believe everyone in this church is sad to see him leave, even if it is for a new ministry on the mission field! And of course, the congregation, the staff, the parents, and the kids are all anxious to know who will be filling the children's pastorate position. As senior pastor, I want to see this season of growth, this momentum continue! You understand that I want to stay on this track we are on, with very little change, and make this the smoothest transition we possibly can. Now, of course, your name came up in our board meetings, Joshua, due to the fact that you've spent the last 2 years interning under and being mentored by Pastor Alan. No one knows our leaders, parents, and kids, and the DNA of Zion Church better than you, Joshua! You practically grew up in this church! Bringing in someone from outside would bring its own set of challenges, and we don't really want to run the risk of changing the "flavor" of our kids' program when things are going so well. Our major concerns with offering this position to you, Joshua, is the fact that you are still in school, newly married, and that at your age, only 23, we do wonder how the parents and volunteers will accept your leadership. But after much thought, prayer, and soul searching, Joshua, we are excited to offer you the position of children's pastor here at Zion Church. What are your thoughts right now Joshua? Joshua?"

Joshua swallowed hard. Wow. He hoped they couldn't see the sweat soaking through his Zion's Kids T-shirt. Could everyone in this room hear his heart thumping? What he was feeling wasn't really fear. He was elated. For almost the entire two years that he had worked with Pastor Alan, Joshua dreamed of this moment—the moment that he—Pastor Joshua—would get to take on the reins of this growing kids' ministry he loved so much! He had desperately hoped that Pastor Alan would wait just another year or two before going on the mission field, so that he would have just a bit longer to finish his degree and gain a bit more credibility with the parents. When Pastor Alan announced he was leaving, Joshua wrestled with his thoughts: "They won't consider me for children's pastor due to my young age, even with Pastor Alan's recommendation, or they'll reject me because I haven't finished my degree yet, or they'll put me on probation until the parents think I'm ready … or worse. They'll bring in an unknown children's pastor, one who will change everything Pastor Alan and I built. Then, this new guy will see me as a threat and make me leave … the pain of that would be unimaginable." But that was then. This was now. Here in the pastor's office, he and the board were offering Joshua his dream on a silver platter.

"Joshua?" Pastor said. "Would you like some time to think and pray about it? And talk to your wife Amy?" Joshua cleared his throat. "No, Amy and I have been thinking and praying about this for awhile and hoping for the opportunity to serve on staff at Zion Church. I'd be honored to accept."

"Fantastic! Joshua, I'm thrilled and excited at what God is doing in our church. In the coming days, we'll be talking more, but I want you to start thinking and praying about this transition. We want it to be as smooth as possible. What do you think are a few things you will need to tackle first? As pastor, I would like you to get together with the parents and volunteers and find out what they need. Really wrap your arms around them; we cannot lose those leaders! Oh, and I would really like you to pull together a task force to start the designs for the upcoming renovation of the children's worship areas and classrooms. We started all that under Pastor Alan, and people have been so excited. I am hopeful you can see that project through. This is going to be a great time for all of us!"

Joshua's head spun. Wow, that was a lot of work that he hadn't thought about. He had only been thinking about all the kids' sermons he would preach and all the fun game nights he wanted to do. Oh well, there would be time for all of that! No dampening his excitement right now!" Of course, Pastor. I'm ready to get on it." They shook hands and closed in prayer.

Joshua left the pastor's office floating on cloud nine. He couldn't wait to move into HIS new office ... to be introduced to the congregation as PASTOR Joshua! Oh wow, that sounded great. He had put in the work. He had earned this moment and now he was stopping to savor it.

Little did Joshua know how difficult that next few weeks and months were going to be for him. Little did he know how ill prepared he was for what he was walking into. It really would have helped Joshua a lot if he had known some of these myths and tips about pastoral transitions.

Common Misconceptions about Transitions in Church Leadership

MYTH 1: NOTHING IS GOING TO CHANGE WITH THIS CHANGE IN LEADERSHIP. EVERYTHING WILL STAY THE SAME.
Truth: Be HONEST with the leaders, the church, the volunteers, and with yourself.

There WILL be change. Change occurs all the time, with any growth, leadership transitions, and time. During a transition in any part of the church leadership team there will be changes. I actually sat in a church service and heard a pastor promise the congregation that "absolutely nothing would change" when his successor came in the next week. In fact, he said, "They wouldn't even be able to tell the difference or even that he had left." Internally, I groaned. He had just promised the church something that could never be delivered. And within a very few short weeks, people were angry and complaining that "things felt different" and "the new guy wants to do something new." I don't believe in making promises to your leaders, parents, and kids that you can't keep. Also, it isn't fair to whoever is coming in! That person will have their own style, giftings, and ministry. It's wrong to expect them to be someone else, or to keep someone else's ministry on life support indefinitely. God will use that new leader and their giftings in wonderful new ways. During a time of transition, it is so important for everyone to stay flexible and to hold their expectations loosely. Don't promise that nothing will change. Promise that you are all doing your best to make this a smooth transition. Promise to care about your leaders, your parents, and your kids. Promise that what matters to them, matters to you. Promise to find (or be) the very best leader you can possibly be and to listen and obey God the best you can, each and every week. And make sure to keep those promises.

MYTH 2: I SHOULD JUMP IN TO CHANGE THINGS, IMMEDIATELY, AS MUCH AS POSSIBLE, WITHOUT LISTENING TO THOSE IN THE TRENCHES AND THOSE WHO WERE THERE BEFORE.
Truth: Smart leaders wait, watch, and listen a lot at first.

Listen to parents, volunteers, staff, and perhaps even your predecessor. I thought I would jump out of my skin waiting to make changes at my last children's pastorate, but we kicked off programs with quality and impact instead of throwing them together. I was so glad we waited and prepared. One of the biggest mistakes a leader can make is going in like a wrecking ball and bowling over people in your wake. Those people are not "in the way of your ministry"; they are your ministry. Most lead pastors have recurrent nightmares about getting a new children's leader who barges in, offends people, causes solid long-term leaders to quit and parents to complain. Yes, you WILL need to make changes, and some people are not going to like them. But take the time up front to build relationships and vision cast. That way, when it's time to take that ministry further, much of your team will be on board with you for the long haul.

MYTH 3: I CAN GAIN MORE CREDIBILITY BY DISCREDITING MY PREDECESSOR.
Truth: Never ever, ever tear down the one before you.

1. There will always be some people—parents, volunteers, and staff, who did like and connect with your predecessor, no matter how things were when they left. It is not worth it to alienate those people. They highly supported the last pastor and may just support you, too.

2. You set the tone of your ministry there. If you set a note of tearing people down, they'll tear you down too eventually. Set a tone of love and encouragement from the start.

3. You do not have all the sides of the story. You may find after a year or two, you agree with the last guy now, and you'll have to eat those words.

4. If there had been a scandal, or the former pastor left on a bad note, don't keep associating yourself and your ministry with that scandal by constantly bringing it up (tearing them down). Make a break with it.

5. Your biggest job right now will be to gain the trust of other staff/parents you may cross paths with. No one is going to trust someone who is putting others down.

6. Putting down the former pastor doesn't make you look better; it makes you look more insecure. You do not need to break anyone's loyalty to a former pastor. Be glad they appreciate and miss the one who left. Then build a ministry they can appreciate and be excited about right now.

MYTH 4: I NEED TO SHOW EVERYONE WHAT I'M MADE OF. I NEED TO DEMAND THAT THEY RESPECT ME AS A LEADER. I WILL PROVE I AM GREAT AT THIS.

Truth: In this day and age, respect is no longer given simply by virtue of the title "pastor."

So many pastors have fallen or acted terribly that, in most cases, you'll have to spend a lot of time and effort earning the trust and respect of the people you serve. However, much more important than proving yourself is:

1. Networking. This is not the time to "hot dog it," as a one-person show. The biggest part of your job will actually involve connecting and working with parents, volunteers, and the other staff. Ask yourself: Who are the key influencers in my area of ministry?

Who are the natural leaders that people in the church are already following? I would advise you to befriend those people, listen to them and their ideas, then, get them on your team working with you.

2. Effective Communicating. Transitions do take a lot of wisdom, so don't let someone see this leadership transition as an opportunity to hijack the whole thing and take over. Don't ever leave a leadership gap that others feel they have to step in and fill. A lot of very gifted pastors leave ministry every year, because they "don't play nice with others." Your giftings will only get you so far.

3. Be Organized. More and more churches are looking for administrative giftings in the children's area and, above all, skill in training up NEW leaders. First impressions matter; do not let your congregation see you as sloppy, unsure, or ill-prepared. Come in organized and ready to go. Don't let age hold you back. Young or old or in the middle, lead with humility and respect for others. Time and hard work are really the only way to earn respect. Stay in there and don't give up! Your ability to work with and connect with others will make or break your ministry. Count on it.

MYTH 5: THE PASTOR EXPLAINED TO THE CONGREGATION THAT I AM A WHOLE NEW KIND OF KIDS' PASTOR, SO I WON'T BE COMPARED TO THE LAST ONE(S).

Truth: Just know that you WILL be compared to the last children's pastor(s).

You will just have to get over that. Be secure in what God called YOU to do. Yes, you will inevitably hear: "I liked the way they did _____better. Why don't you do _____? You can't repaint that wall mural! _____ designed that! I liked their curriculum better." It's human nature. No matter how well you do, there will always be some people who connected with and liked the last leader and everything they did. That's just the way it is. You just keep focusing on doing what God is leading you to do with a lot of grace, love, and passion. You cannot make everyone happy (though some of us have a really hard time with that).

MYTH 6: I AM FOLLOWING A GREAT CHILDREN'S PASTOR IN A WONDERFUL MINISTRY PROGRAM, SO THIS TRANSITION WILL BE SO EASY.

Truth: Know that for some, change of any kind is not easy.

Even the best of transitions will have bumps along the way. And it may appear that these problems didn't happen until you came on. You have to find your own identity, possibly without your mentor. Who are you as a leader? As a children's pastor? Sometimes that takes a little time to figure out.

MYTH 7: WE SHOULD GIVE OUT AS LITTLE INFORMATION AS POSSIBLE. PEOPLE JUST HAVE TO TRUST THE LEADERSHIP DURING TRANSITION. THE LESS THEY KNOW THE BETTER.

Truth: You're going to need to communicate over and over and over in many ways and very clearly.

If you don't, people will insert their own interpretation. I left to speak at a conference a little while back and didn't feel the need to talk about it a lot at our church. All of a sudden I started getting texts at the arena, "Are you really leaving the church?" Then, "Are you pregnant?" And finally, "Praying you get healed of your cancer. Don't give up!" I laughed a bit, but it also scared me. How quickly people's perceptions can be influenced if you do not give enough of the "right" information. No, I wasn't leaving the church, I wasn't pregnant, and I definitely wasn't in end-stage cancer, but that's just how the rumor mill can run. Without giving out too much information, you need to communicate effectively and efficiently the crucial details of the ministry transition in order to keep your team with you. It's no longer, "I say and you do without questions." Now it must become, "Let's minister to these kids and families as a team. Let's decide and clearly outline the steps we need to take to reach our goals."

What about the really tough transitions? What if the previous pastor/leader fell, had a major scandal, or was arrested? Or what if the church leadership fired your predecessor whom everyone loved or everyone hated? What about when the leader before you left on really bad terms or ran the ministry into the ground? What if you weren't the first choice for your position?

Anytime you're going into a really tough transition, you're going to have to do everything in the tips above ... only more so. You're going to have to listen more, love more, wait longer, work harder, network stronger, forgive more often. Remember, you're dealing with a special, yet not that uncommon, situation that calls for tender loving care. Everything we just talked about will be greatly intensified. Emotion will be running high. Trust may have been demolished and will take a lot longer to rebuild (some may never trust you). These families and volunteers will be less likely to step up and try new things, wary of getting onboard. But remember how Jesus handles His children who are broken, *"A bruised reed He will not break, a smoldering ember He will not put out."* Sometimes God calls us to the truly tough trenches and that takes a very special pastor. These situations grow us the most, and no situation is perfect.

What if you're coming in from outside that specific church? Well, hiring from the outside has its advantages: no favoritism, usually a more qualified person, an untainted outside perspective. And it has its disadvantages: a children's pastor from outside the church may be completely unfamiliar with the culture of the community or the church. They won't already know the people, the kids, the parents, or the leaders. They will have to wait longer to make major changes and work harder to earn credibility and respect. If you're being hired from outside the church, you'll have to focus more than an insider on learning the culture and networking with the people of the church. That will have to be your priority one!

MYTH 8: LEADERS CAN COME AND GO, BUT IF OUR SYSTEMS ARE GREAT, IT WON'T MATTER. IT'LL BE FINE AND NO ONE WILL NOTICE.
Truth: Too much turnover is a red flag.

Systems cannot replace anointed leaders. Everyone does have a "flavor." But these days, most people don't want faceless corporations; they want a face. Don't minimize the problems caused by frequent transitions. Don't excuse them. Find out why so many departures are happening and then do what it takes to build stability in your staff and key volunteers, especially for the sake of the kids and families! A very good children's pastor friend of mine once said, "You have to be at a church at least 3 years to make any real difference there at all." In most cases, I would have to agree. So build an environment that encourages longevity in the staff and key volunteers. If you're the leader, do not leave without a lot of thought and prayer. Don't be impatient or frustrated early on. There's a lot to be said for staying power!

MYTH 9: WE DID THINGS SO WELL IN THIS TRANSITION THAT WE WON'T LOSE ANYONE AT ALL!
Truth: Even if you do everything perfectly, some will leave.

It's just a fact. But the goal is still to grow. Don't take it personally, and don't let it discourage you. The people who leave may have just been too connected to the previous pastor, or burned out and looking for anyone else to be in charge so they could finally leave. Poorly handled, you can have a disastrous exodus of great people, taking years to recover from. Your goal here is to minimize the loss of people and not to make it worse (see tips above).

I highly suggest swallowing any and all pride and asking the people who leave why they are leaving (exit interviews). This can really help you find and correct problems before they blow up bigger. Do not get "short" with people who decide to leave. Extend them love and grace, always leaving the door wide open for them to come back. Then, when your team and plan are in place, you'll be ready to grow!

What if you are transitioning in as the new children's leader? Here are a few questions you need to ask and have carefully answered before you accept a ministry position.

Is this church looking for a children's pastor or children's leader/administrator?

Before accepting the position you should know if the job description is for a pastor, an administrator, or a bit of both. Job descriptions are important. When I look through children's pastor/director job descriptions I see many terms (buzz words) like "cutting edge", "relational", "team player", "family minister", "creative", "leader of leaders", "self starter who can hit the ground running", and "not a one-man (or woman) show." More and more churches, especially larger churches, are looking for more of an administrator to head up their programs for children's ministry instead of a pastor. The sheer volume of details involved with coordinating that many children needs a "Joseph" (or several of them) with a lot of wisdom and great organizational skills. What is the difference really? Which one does your church really need or want to hire? Which one are you? Here's how to tell.

A Children's Pastor provides leadership, vision, strategy, recruitment, coordinates teams of volunteers and parents. He/she has a background/training in pastoral work/studies. The position or role is a pastoral role. This person sits on the pastoral leadership team and has direct input and influence on the direction and future of the children's ministries department as a whole. As a pastor, this person baptizes, visits homes and hospitals, etc.— has a pastoral ministry calling.

A Children's Director is a person who works more on the administrative side of things. Usually a previous children's pastor or the current lead pastor or pastoral leadership team have already provided the vision and direction for the children's department, and the children's director is the person in the trenches carrying out that plan. The children's director typically does not have a background in pastoral ministry and may have limited influence on the direction and future (curriculum, budget, recruitment strategies) for the kids' ministry department.

Names matter. Influence matters. It is mission critical that your understanding of your role is crystal clear before you sign on the dotted line and step into that ministry. Expectations matter. If your church is expecting a children's "pastor", but you do not want to do baby dedications, baptisms, kids' worship, etc., you may have an awkward clash of expectations. Or if your church thought they wanted a visionary, strong leader and communicator/children's pastor, but what they really wanted was a very organized administrator to carry on all of the programs that the former children's pastor had instituted, this is going to lead to problems.

During the interview process ask these questions.

1. Are you looking for someone to provide vision or to carry out a pre-existing vision? If this position is a director position and will be managing a pre-existing vision, who came up with the vision, and who is setting that vision now? (former children's pastor, senior leader, Family Life Director, a curriculum?)

2. Who chooses the curriculum we use? Am I locked into the current one? If so, for how long? Who would have to approve a curriculum change?

3. What is your church's policy on providing childcare for events? Would I be responsible for recruiting/providing childcare for church events? How many events are there per month?

4. Does the church do evangelism/outreach? (Not all do!) What and how many outreaches and serving opportunities does the church do and how would I be involved?

5. What expectations would the church have for my spouse/children?

6. What is the typical work schedule/hours for staff members?

7. What is the senior leader's vision for the children's department? This is crucial, because his/her vision for that area is automatically your vision, which you must uphold and defend. If you accept that position, the senior leader's vision is your ultimate ceiling for how far you can go in your ministry at that church.

8. What is the church's official position on women in ministry? This is good to know whether you are a male or female applicant. A male worship pastor friend of mine was shocked when the church did not support his wife going for credentials.

9. How many staff members have they had (total in all areas) come in and go out over the past 3 years? If there was a huge turnover at one point, what was the reason?

10. What were the circumstances of the last children's leader's departure?

11. Who would I be directly reporting to? If I have a problem or a question will I go to the senior leader or a family life director or elder? What you are really asking is: Who is your boss on a day-to-day basis? You may adore the lead pastor, but really, really have a rough experience working for his wife.

After your get your questions answered, here are a few more things to do before accepting a position.

1. Do your homework! It is not a bad idea to do a Google search on the church you are interviewing with. You may be surprised what pops up. I researched one, and the first thing that popped up was "child sex scandal", from just one year ago. Right before that, they'd had an embezzlement crime that made national news. They had, unfortunately, failed to mention any of that. What you find may not change your mind if you truly feel called to that church and that place, but I believe it's good to know as much as possible. Make an informed decision and go in with your eyes open.

2. Talk to former staff members that left under great circumstances and ones who may have been asked to leave. Again, it may not change your mind, but it's good to get a complete picture.

3. Find out as much as you can about the history of the church, their doctrine and practices, the culture of the area, and the culture of the church.

4. If possible, talk to your district, denomination, presbytery, etc. and see if they can give you any insight on the church.

5. Beware of accepting a position on the promise that "When things are better, we will pay you, give you an office, give you benefits." Usually once you accept the position, those promises do not come to be. They already have you, and you were willing to do it for free. If you go to a church to serve, do it because you are called, but know that not all of those promises to get you there may actually happen.

LAST THOUGHT

How do I know if it's my time to make a transition (leave my current position)?

1. You just don't care anymore. You cannot shake apathy. Something doesn't go well, or you exceed goals—and it doesn't faze you either way. Something inside you has died for this ministry.

2. You are almost always frustrated, irritated, and resentful. It's perfectly normal to be frustrated at times (especially Mondays)! If these feelings of anger, hurt, and resentment have gone on and on and nothing you're doing is helping, it may be time for you to leave before that attitude gets worse and/or poisons those around you.

3. Vision is gone. You are no longer hoping or planning for great things a long way off for the ministry there. You can barely focus on planning for this coming Sunday. Planning for a year from now is nearly impossible, because you can no longer see the future for this ministry. Writing messages further out is becoming more difficult.

4. You find yourself often daydreaming about a different ministry/church. A lot of leaders dream of one day filling in for Francis Chan on a Sunday and 2000 people get saved. But if all you do is hope and dream about another ministry, then your heart may have died for this one. That's not fair for the people at your current church.

5. You are now there for the wrong reasons—money, habit, fear. You do not want to be there at all, but you just don't know how to do anything else. Or you're afraid of going somewhere new, which leads to a great question:

Why are you staying? _____

Ministry is always a balancing act that takes a lot of wisdom. Don't stay too short a time and hurt people, while cheating the work God was trying to do. But don't stay too long and cheat the work that God is about to do—in you, in your current ministry, and in your future ministry.

Our God is the same yesterday, today, and forever, but He is also very skilled at handling transitions. Scripture is full of big changes. Let's trust the Lord of these ministrychanges,while attempting to handle them with wisdom and sensitivity. Then we can truly get excited about what God is doing in His churches.

(See the back of this book for sample exit interview questions!)

CHAPTER 2:
THE CREATIVE WORSHIP SPACE

"I can just see it now. A sharp, cutting-edge kids' area with a lot of cool stuff that kids and new families will love! We will grow so fast." Pastor was so animated. Joshua was excited, too. Pastor's ideas were exhilarating. Both of them couldn't wait to get started renovating the kids' areas. Joshua was writing as fast as he could, trying to keep up with Pastor's rapid fire ideas. Pastor was using big hand motions. "We need to have a lot of cool stuff. Um. Like treehouse check-in stations! Yeah. Treehouses would be great."

Joshua's head snapped up. "Wait, what? Where would we get ..."

"And stuff that looks like Disney rides. That's what we need," Pastor continued.

Joshua was struggling to catch up, "Um, Disney rides? I don't know how ... can we go back to the treehouse thing?"

"And you know what Joshua?" said Pastor, not hearing him yet. "The board and I recently visited a large church out of state, and do you know what they had?"

Joshua stammered, "I … I really have no idea." This was starting to feel overwhelming.

"Slides! Yeah, slides going into every classroom. Wouldn't that be great? We would love to see slides in your plan. Oh, and maybe some trees all around the infant nursery. Oh! And please make sure that all of this is safe for the kids. This is going to be great!"

"Ah … um … okay." Pastor Joshua was not feeling that it would be great. He had a sour, tight feeling in the pit of his stomach as he tried to figure out how he would make all of this a reality. Surely a real children's pastor could create all of this. Or are you supposed to buy it? And from where?

Still smiling, Pastor slid a piece of paper with an amount written on it, across the table. "This is how much your predecessor budgeted for the renovations, and it is too late in the year to change that now, but I am sure you can do a lot with this."

With a fresh burst of involuntary thrill, Joshua thought, "Hey, this could be fun. I will figure out a way to make this amazing. Let's see what I have to work with." But as he turned the piece of paper over, the amount on the paper seemed like a joke. He desperately thought, "This is almost nothing. What can I do? Where do I even start? Where do I look? Who do I ask? And he wants treehouses? And … slides? The only thing I know for sure right now is I'm in a lot of trouble."

I actually sat in on a meeting like this once. Where do you start? If you're interested in upgrading or updating your kids' ministry space, it can truly seem like a daunting task. But like everything else in ministry, we need to go back to your vision, and carefully craft a plan before knocking down walls or grabbing paintbrushes. Facility changes, especially those that will be a considerable investment for the church, should be carefully thought through. You want your updates to fit your church's vision, to be functional, sustainable, and still allow for and assist with your growth.

What is the purpose behind upgrading your kids' ministry spaces? Well, first of all, did you know that your space speaks? No space is mute. If you've been there awhile, though, you may not be listening to what your facility is saying anymore. I've chosen not to eat at certain restaurants before because when I walked in, the space said, "We do not clean. We do not have enough staff. This is not important enough to us to update anything. Your meal is probably not going to matter to us either."

And what is your kids' space saying about your kids' ministry? What is it saying about your vision and passion for kids? What does it say about your church's real feeling about kids' ministry? Does it say, "Exciting! Fun! Our family ministries are important to us"? Or does your space shout to new parents, "We babysit kids in a dark, dusty, dirty, cluttered area, far away from 'real church.' What we're doing is not very important to us, because your kids are not that important to us. We do not bother updating anything. We're throwing this together. This will be dull, so sit and be quiet"?

Answer this question for me honestly. If I were to look at your kids' areas right now, would I think that you are allowing kids into your ministry or that you are welcoming them, their families, and their friends? Would I think that you're excited for them to be there? This is all part of the enormous job we get to be a part of each week. It's the most important job in the world: setting up a meeting—a play date—between kids and their Father in heaven. A room for that kind of meeting should be pretty special.

With that in mind, what elements do we need to take into consideration when planning our family ministry space upgrades? What do we need to plan for and prioritize?

1. Safety. I hope you'll see the safety chapter in my first book, *Your Children's Ministry From Scratch*. A great place to meet with God must be a safe place. Safety must be priority one when planning your spaces. If a design element comes down to safety versus fun, safety always trumps. This includes planning where the entrances and exits should be and limiting how many of them there are. Your ultimate goal is to have as much of a "secured children's wing" as possible. Go through the Facilities Safety Checklist in book one and refer back to it often as you refurbish your space.

2. Color. Are your kids' ministry areas drab and dull? Kids love bright colors. Just check out Nickelodeon, Disney XD, and MineCraft. Paint is relatively cheap and easy to change, but it can make a huge difference in the way your space feels. Want an inexpensive way to shake things up? Buy some paint, get some very skilled leaders, and make your kids' areas feel like brand new. If your areas have been that way awhile, or someone painted a lot of murals in there, you may have a bit of trouble getting approval. But, paint colors and murals were never meant to last forever. Letting them stay too long may hold your ministry back by repelling new families. The right new colors will create excitement, because they tell people, "Something new is happening here." Your space needs to reflect the excitement in your programs!

3. Child-Friendly. I realize that many churches have multi-purpose spaces that are for children's ministry some days and adult classes on other days. These churches are often resistant to allowing any child-friendly paint, wall décor, or design elements to these rooms because, "the adults have to meet here, too." They think they're saving money and problems by making everything in their building vanilla and generic. The problem with this is that in our child-centric culture, most families simply expect designated children's spaces almost everywhere they go. Doctor's offices, libraries, restaurants, and gyms all have child-friendly areas to attract more families. Blank spaces merely say, "We are tolerating your kids in our adult classrooms during these services, but they had better not wreck anything." Here is the cold hard truth: Multi-purpose space is just adult classroom space. Adults already have the main sanctuary and the entire rest of the building. Another truth: adults really can meet in kids' classrooms. It really won't kill them. Most of them don't mind at all. However, kids can have trouble meeting in adult spaces, and in fact, it may not even be safe.

What if you are currently part of a church plant, portable church, site church, or a kids' church that absolutely must share space? (More on that in just a minute.) Bottom line: No matter what space you have (theater, school, 100-year-old building), churches should always work toward creating spaces that welcome children and families, from where they park their car, to the entrances they use, to the welcome/check-in stations, to the "main event" … all the way to checkout.

On a scale of 1-10, with 10 being the best, most welcoming family ministry facility ever, what would you rate your children's areas? _____

Why did you give it that number? _____
_____

Now I want you to ask someone outside your ministry area, preferably a brand new visitor, to rate it the same way. Tell them to be honest!

_____
_____

How did the two numbers/assessments compare? Were you surprised by anything? Remember not to get emotional or defensive. We're always looking for ways to improve the way we communicate God's love, and our facility is part of that.

4. Lighting. Lighting can change the whole feel of a room. I highly suggest you get someone with experience to come in and give you options for your space. I worked with one church that used multi-purpose rooms. They painted the stages in each room black, and then used different colored lighting to set the scene. It was amazing! Whether adults, students, or children met in that room, the effect was energizing and exciting. Children's areas should have creative, fun lighting, and think colors. I do a lot with black light, strobe lights, color gel cannons and more. Just be careful to consider your special needs children—autistic and epileptic children especially—when choosing your lighting for a weekend (see chapter 4). I have a volunteer (a student) who works solely with our creative lighting. It takes our services to a whole new level.

Walk through your pre-k and nursery areas. How old are those fixtures? How can you plan to update your fixtures and your lighting? You will be amazed at how lighting can change the whole look and feel of a space for very little money.

5. Flooring. Is your flooring safe? Is it freezing cold concrete? Is it ripped up and tattered carpeting that should be mercifully shot, buried, and given a hasty funeral? We have priced and ordered carpeting before, and if you get a deal on it, it's not too cost prohibitive, especially if you can get volunteers to help you with installation. Again, that one change can make a huge difference in the perceived value of your kids' ministry. Think fun, modern colors! Or you may want to look at laminate flooring or tile, which is much easier to clean if a child vomits or you have a spill. Our pre-k leaders have requested a change to laminate in all of our pre-k rooms, because it looks sharp and professional and is so easy to clean. If you get a quality laminate or tile floor, it will last you for a while and go with many different paint changes. If it's concrete, can you paint it? Anything to liven up bare concrete is a plus in my book.

6. Location. You may or may not have a lot of influence on where your kids' programs meet. By and large, I'm not a fan of putting kids in a dark basement. (That can be a fire hazard, also). If you get the chance to have input in location decisions, try to get your nurseries as close to the main sanctuary as possible. New parents are reluctant to have their baby out of arms' reach. If you want parents to use your nursery, keep it close to your main sanctuary. At the same time, if your elementary service is like mine, it may do better with some space in between them and the other services. We get loud and crazy in worship, games, and occasional giving challenges. I do not like shushing the kids all morning. I want them to have fun and be kids!

7. Technology. Is it time to upgrade your sound and tech? Probably! Look at adding mics, or a new mixer, an iPad with stand, check-in systems, and/or self check-in stations. If you're upgrading your rooms, then now is the time to plan to upgrade your tech. The cost of some technology, including new sound systems, may be less than you think! This is probably going to be the largest expense you will have with renovating, so get some help in choosing well! Technology in your children's ministry is never something you can check off your list; it's never done. If I were to write you a thorough list here of the brand new advances in kids' ministry technology, all of those tips would be obsolete by the time this went to print. There are always advances happening (daily), and to be effective in your ministry, you're going to need to stay on top of them. I highly recommend having an IT person and/or a young tech savvy person on your renovation team.

8. Guest Appeal. Remember how families decide in the first 10 minutes if they will ever come back? They still haven't heard your kids worship or tried out your church's coffee bar or been through a single object lesson. What they did have time to see in those crucial 10 minutes was your greeters, your check-in process and … (drumroll here) your kids' space! No pressure, no pressure. What many churches ignore is their check-in area, which may be the most important area to keep sharp and updated. Don't skimp when decorating this area. Is it colorful and bright? Does it make new families feel welcome and even excited for what's to come in your services?

9. Storage. Even if I've never met you and have never visited your church, I already know that you do not have enough storage. In all of your facility planning, you're probably not planning for enough storage space. Every church seems to have this problem! You need to start now in the planning process to provide storage space. No matter how much storage you create, you will probably fill it in a matter of weeks. This means you'll need to constantly plan for team "storage room purging and organizing days." We do ours right after our fall family outreach and again after Easter. Don't waste time totally cleaning and organizing your storage areas before or during an outreach (parade, VBS, sports camp); we know that's when your storage areas will be packed and perhaps chaotic. Let's be honest! Right after the outreach, though, is a great time for a purge. Be a bit ruthless in deciding what stays and what needs to go. No one has the space to keep everything. Consider donating your older items to a missionary work or a start-up church in your area. Find a kids' ministry you can trade items with—sets, puppets, lights, curriculum. This blesses both ministries' budgets and drastically cuts down on your storage needs. In all your planning for renovating your areas, don't forget to plan for storage space!

Hopefully, the ideas above haven't overwhelmed you yet. So once you know what to look for, how do you get started making your ideas for that stellar ministry area a reality?

First, you need a few objective outside perspectives. This is a big job and calls for a creative team of people. I highly recommend you handpick your task force to get several opinions and viewpoints, but always reserve the final call to be between you and your senior leader. I would not make the final product up for a vote. Who should be on your task force? Look for a couple of parents, a safety expert (police officer, fire fighter), a daycare worker/supervisor (to give you great ideas), and possibly a children's pastor consultant from a nearby church. Identify first what you must have to operate safely and effectively. If it comes down to a design element versus safety, remember that safety always trumps fun.

Secondly, you must, together with your senior leader and your team, identify your ministries' top needs. What are the main issues you need to address by this renovation? For example, when we decided to renovate our kids' areas, our top five facility upgrades included: 1. sharper, professional signage throughout the kids' wing; 2. an exciting, vibrant area for pre-k large group worship; 3. an easily identifiable new guest check-in area that was warm, modern, and welcoming; 4. more classroom space for our growing early childhood area; and 5. a larger stage for the elementary large group space that would accommodate our new kids' live worship team.

Another church I worked with had these five goals: 1. get rid of all asbestos, and safely replace all lead paint with fresh bright colors; 2. move the elementary group from the basement to the fellowship hall, and build a portable sharp set for them to use on Sundays and Wednesdays; 3. streamline the flow of traffic through check-in and checkout, and create one-way entrances and exits; 4. repair heating ducts in the pre-k rooms; and 5. purchase new colorful, age-appropriate seating for all classrooms.

Based on what we've learned so far, what would you say are the top five facility issues that your church needs to address in a children's ministry facility renovation?

1. _____
2. _____
3. _____
4. _____
5. _____

Take your time figuring these out, as the goals above should set the tone and direction for all of your renovations.

Thirdly, do your homework! Jesus said that it is wise before starting a project to sit down and count the cost. And it makes sense to know your options and take the time to get it done right and well, so as to avoid having to redo your work or do it all again too soon. A facilities renovation is a massive undertaking; please do not underestimate the amount of time and money involved. This is people's tithe money! That thought should help us plan soberly and with great intentionality. What will meet your goals/needs? What can you really afford? What can we do right now, and what can wait for another year?

How should you go about doing your homework on creating an amazing kids' ministry space? Here are some tips.

It's time for a field trip. Pack up that team, and leave church property. You need to visit a few churches with amazing kids' ministry stages and facilities. Not everything they do will work at your church or even be applicable with your programs, but you'll get great ideas for your own building. If you call ahead, most churches will even give you a tour and let you ask questions! Also go visit newer schools, children's theaters, Disney on Ice, and amusement parks. Inspiration can be found just about anywhere! Write down all the great ideas you're getting.

Consider your options. If you look online, you can find several businesses that will come in and design your area for you. This is certainly the most expensive and arguably the gold standard for kids' creative environments. Check out websites like worldsofwow.com and you will see what I mean. When I go there, I have to repent of covetousness every time. It costs so much because they fly in to your church, assess your facility, give you options, and then they build an environment for you that would rival any theme park. It's called Worlds of Wow for a reason! If you're blessed enough to have designated kids' ministry space that you are free to decorate, then you may want to invest in having a professional create a masterpiece for you. You may also want to look into more local, cheaper options. We found a local artist who did all of our classroom spaces, doors, bathrooms, and more for a fraction of the cost of bringing in a larger company. Don't be afraid to get a team of talented volunteers from your own church and do a work day to update painting, etc. You're always limited to schedules and personal giftings when using volunteers, but find out what talent you already have in your midst.

Designated Kids' Space. One of the drawbacks of designated kids' church space is that your renovations need to be long term commitments. The monetary and time investment for renovating a permanent space is considerable. This means you should be planning to use your new renovation for at least five years. You'll have to be creative after the first year, keeping the environment fresh and exciting. I would not recommend making the theme of your permanent space anything trendy or currently popular; don't pattern it after one curriculum (most become obsolete within a few years). This will ensure that you get the maximum mileage on your investment for years to come!

Portable Church, Multi-Purpose and Shared Kids' Church Space. I would like to take a moment and thank my friend, Children's Pastor Ken Neff, for providing pictures of his creations for children's church stages, pictures that I have included throughout this chapter. The reason I included his work is that he, his wife, and team have created these outstanding kids' church environments for little to no money. That's right! They took almost no budget— just creativity, volunteer muscle, and a lot of passion—to build a space that makes kids excited to meet with God! I asked Ken to share a bit for all of us on how we can build an awe-inspiring kids' church environment on a budget. Here's what he had to say.

"We like to teach, train and equip children ministry leaders that the aspect of changing your environment can be done with proper planning without changing the budget Both my wife, Andrea, and I are dedicated to empowering other leaders in many ways, but feel that God has placed creativity on the forefront of our training.

All of the designs are God-inspired, by looking at everyday things kids can relate to and making them cohesive with the Bible. Disney captures our imaginations with the "Wow" factor, so why can't we as the church do the same? Either the world is going to capture their attention or the church will, so think big, dream big, and ask God to help with creativity. After all, look at what He's created and is still doing today.

I think stage design is very important for the church and especially children's ministry because the designs tell a story and give the children a visual taste of what your church is all about. Is it traditional, contemporary, series minded, fun or just plain out of the box as it relates to their worship experience. We are wired to be visually stimulated, whether it's the food we eat, the cars we buy, or the common recognition through TV commercials and ads. This starts as babies when we are mesmerized by the mobile placed above the crib. So when a stage design is well thought out with color, instrument placement, props, graphics, video, and lighting, it brings it all together for God's glory. When making God's house eye appealing and relational to people, don't be afraid to change it up from time to time. Give it a fresh look and think out of the box.

We create monthly themes to go along with the curriculum that we write so it all goes together; however, you can take any curriculum or story and make it come alive through a visual concept.

A portable church can create props and stages by thinking thin. It's not just thin on the budget, but thin meaning that you use lightweight wooden or wire frames and materials such as Styrofoam sheets, cardboard, and plywood. Since movability and storage is key in portable churches, measure your storage space so you don't get carried away with size. You can always lift your props off the floor to create the illusion of a bigger piece.

I wish I could tell you I had a massive budget; however, I'm like the rest of you in ministry, I have a small budget, too. I suggest the budget has to be modified to your specific needs in children's ministry and naturally half of it cannot go for props. A good rule that I go by is

I wish I could tell you I had a massive budget; however, I'm like the rest of you in ministry, I have a small budget, too. I suggest the budget has to be modified to your specific needs in children's ministry and naturally half of it cannot go for props, so a good rule that I go by is 10-20% for stage and props. I know what most are thinking—that's not much, but that's where planning and thinking outside the box play a big roll. And of course praying for God's provision is always number one in my book. He doesn't have a budget, so ask God and watch what He can do."
-Ken Neff, Children's Pastor, Christ Central Church, Lake City, Florida

Thank you so much for inspiring us, Ken! Check out his Facebook page to see more examples of his work.

I think we can see now that our creativity should never be held back by budgets, space, or portability. Your space speaks. What is your space saying this weekend? Let's do the work, bring in our team,s and craft a space that makes every child and every family say, "Wow!" Let's set them up for the experience of meeting with God—an experience that will change the course of their lives forever. That should make all of us say, "Wow, I'm so glad I get to do this!"

CHAPTER THREE
WHEN TRAGEDY STRIKES—DEALING WITH THE TOUGHEST MINISTRY SITUATIONS

I stared into the mirror in the church's bathroom at my reflection. I looked hilarious in my Dorothy costume, long brown pigtails, blue bows, shiny red shoes, and painted on freckles. I even had the "Toto" puppet on my right arm, all ready to step out on stage. In just a few moments our kids' ministry team, including our student worship team, drama team, and kids' choir would be ministering in our back-to-school outreach in front of almost 1,000 people. We had rehearsed all summer long, planned, trained, advertised, and prayed. And now the moment was here. Everything seemed to be ready. The only thing out of place in this picture was ... the tears pouring down my face, smearing my make-up, drawing long mascara lines down to my chin.

"Hello? Trish? Are you still there? Are you going to tell the kids yet?"

Her question shook me back to reality. I forced my lips to move. "I will definitely have to tell the kids. But I'll wait until the outreach is over tonight. And I am so, so sorry for your loss."

My wonderful assistant children's pastor and dear friend, Sonya Lallemont, who grew up in that church, had only 10 weeks ago been diagnosed with cancer at the young age of 33. Almost every child and teenager in that church had had Sonya for their Sunday school teacher at one time or another. They all knew her from every outreach, rehearsal, and kids' church service we had ever had. My own children called her "aunt." After the initial shock had worn off a little, we banded together as a church to pray earnestly for Sonya, and to support her and her husband. But this was one of the fastest cancers I had ever seen. It was unrelenting and unmerciful. That phone call, right before this outreach, was Sonya's sister calling me to tell me that Sonya had suddenly slipped into a coma and was not expected to live much longer. Somehow, I walked out there, pasted on a smile for a packed house, and we put on the best family outreach we had ever done. The kids sang their hearts out, danced, acted … and they prayed with many of their friends to receive Christ around those altars.

Afterwards, instead of our usual celebrations, in exhaustion, we faced the funeral. Sonya's husband asked the kids' choir to sing at it. I also was asked to speak about my friend and co-worker's life and ministry. Looking out at a full house, I told a story to the congregation about how in days long ago, when a great hero finally marched home from battle, the grateful ones they served would drop roses down to the streets below to show their appreciation and admiration for a battle well fought. When our kids' choir finished singing the worship songs Sonya had taught them, they each, one-by-one, came down from the stage and laid a single rose on her casket until it was overflowing with roses all over the floor. She was a hero to them, coming home from a battle well fought, and we wanted to show our appreciation.

When I sat down in the audience, I expected to get to fall apart on my own. But when I opened my eyes the children had all left their parents' seats and had crowded all around me crying. Their biggest question was, "Why?" This gaping loss had left a hole in all of us.

In the weeks that followed, the questions just kept coming: How do we even begin to minister to these kids and their families? How do we talk to children about dying, death, loss, or eternity? How do we talk to children about trusting God when you pray and pray but God says, "No"? How do you obey God when you do not understand? How do you minister to children and families when you are crushed with grief yourself?

This is one of the most difficult parts of our job. This is one of the things they didn't train me for in Bible college. There is an overwhelming sense of all the things you didn't know that you didn't know. When you first go into ministry, you're excited to get in there doing crazy costumed characters, fun black light puppets, messy games and contests, loud music, and the most cutting edge videos. But the dark truth is that this is the part of the job you will face sooner or later, and then over and over again. You are ministering to people in a broken world. You're ministering to kids who will be exposed to death, divorce, loss, and bullying. And as their minister, you should be present more than ever in times of crisis. This is not the time to pass the buck simply because you are uncomfortable. When I say loss and crisis, I mean divorce as well. Remember, children often react to a divorce much like they would react to any other loss or death in their lives … no way around that. Children of divorce will need love, support, and ministry, too. No other time will mean more to these families than what happens during a time of crisis for them.

So what should you say or do during a time of crisis for a family in your church? I don't have all the answers, but here are a few things I have garnered from experience and some tips from other children's leaders who have lived through times of crisis with their churches. I truly hope these tips help you minister well to families and children in their time of need.

FIRST OF ALL, WHEN A DEATH OR A LOSS/TRAGEDY HAS JUST OCCURRED, DO NOT SAY OR DO THESE THINGS.

"Heaven needed another angel." Despite the obvious theological problems with this statement (humans and angels are not the same creations/species and humans do not turn into angels after death), these words are very trite and insinuate that God took that person or that pet because of heaven's need. This adds to the feeling the child or parent may already be struggling with that says, "God took someone I loved away from me." We can sympathize with someone's pain without saying God had to take that person.

"Too bad they didn't make heaven." Whether or not you personally believe that the deceased person made it to heaven or not, a death or a funeral is not the place to have that discussion. Your focus now has to be on the family of the deceased. You probably do not have all the facts, and some things we will not know for sure until we get to heaven. All such speculation is pointless, and may just hurt rather than help at the funeral. In a divorce situation, do not bash

either parent for any reason. No matter what, that will always be their mother and their father. Love and minister to the child and the family without ripping into either parent.

"This won't be such a big deal in awhile. Just give it time." It is a big deal! No person can ever take the place of another person. Each child, each human, is unique, and there will never be another of that loved one. Let that person recognize and grieve that loss of an individual who is no longer there. For the child of divorce, it IS a big deal, and a huge loss. Do not trivialize a child's loss or any person's loss.

"God doesn't give us more than we can handle." This is a twisting of a scripture in James chapter 5 that tells us that God will not give us more temptation than we can handle. Many times, God allows situations in our lives, for reasons we do not understand, that are far more than we can handle on our own. And it is in these situations that God has to carry us, because we simply cannot handle them in our own strength.

Do not say, "I'm here for you," and then disappear right after the funeral or divorce. In fact, do not say things that you do not mean. It has been well said before that people will not remember much of what you say after a tragedy or at the funeral. But they will remember that you were there. Many times, the comforters dissipate and/or disappear shortly after the funeral meal is over. The time to really be present and show the love of Christ is in the weeks and months and years that follow that funeral or that loss. Say, "I'm here for you" and mean it!

"Well, God took them because …" and "God did this because …" This one probably bothers me the most. As Christians, we are unnerved if we sense someone may be getting upset with God when they are grieving. Listen, we do not need to defend God. We always try to find the "why" in every situation. A child's favorite question is "Why?" Even Jesus asked, "Why?" Sometimes we never know the why this side of heaven, but we're called to trust His love anyway. God is big enough to handle the anger that comes right along with the grief. We shouldn't try to make up desperate explanations to defend God when we do not really understand the situation ourselves.

"Well, we all knew this was coming. They were sick so long, (or your parents were fighting so long) at least you were ready for it." You are never truly ready to lose a loved one no matter how long they have been in crisis. You will still grieve.

"Just think of Job. Your loss isn't that bad then." Misery does not always love company. Pointing out someone else's tragedy probably will not make a family feel better about their loss. And it almost comes off as guilting like, "Your loss isn't nearly as bad as theirs." You cannot compare losses, tragedies, or heartbreaks. Scripture tells us, *"Each heart knows its own bitterness"* (Proverbs 14:10). We all grieve differently. Comparisons don't really help.

"The only grief counseling you need is a Bible and a prayer closet." Scripture and prayer are fantastic, especially during times of grief. But I always point people to grief counseling as well, and that includes children. Most pastors are not trained in grief counseling or trauma intervention. It is wonderful to use scripture, prayer, and counseling, but there are specialists who are trained in these situations and are ready to help. People going through a loss are going to need all the support and all the tools we can give them.

NOW THAT WE TALKED ABOUT WHAT WE SHOULDN'T SAY, WHAT IS IT THAT WE ACTUALLY SHOULD SAY AND DO FOR A GRIEVING PERSON AND FAMILY?

Don't say a whole lot. Be there for them at the time of the tragedy and in the many months to follow. Listen. Give hugs. Do send scriptures and cards. Let them know you are praying for them (and mean it). Being there is so important and not just right after the loss has occurred. When the funeral is over, and the cards have stopped coming, and the relatives have all gone home. and everyone else has moved on … that may be when that person/family needs you the most.

Let them cry. Let them be angry. Relive memories of the lost person with them. Do not shame them for crying and grieving. It's normal; it's a part of life.

Continually point them to Jesus who alone can get them through the unbearable. Be there for them. Eventually, inevitably, you'll need them to be there for you, too. Jesus said, *"Your love for one another will prove you are My disciples"* (Mt. 13:35).

Expect and be prepared for a delayed response from children. In fact, the younger the child is when the loss occurs the more delayed the response will be. And children, like adults, all grieve differently. Many times, they will cry, be angry, laugh, sing, and play all in the same hour. And it's not that they didn't care about the one they lost. Children

oftentimes cannot sustain that level of deep grief for hours at a time, so it comes in waves. Many times their grief shows up in the form of acting out. One child we had in our ministry would repeatedly punch out windows or hit his head into a wall. Finally, his grandmother let us know that the boy found his mother dead of a drug overdose six months prior and had been doing that everywhere ever since. We worked with the family to get the boy counseling and he is doing much better. It sometimes helps to know what is fueling the behavior. Grief has no set timeline. Children especially will have a delayed response. They may suddenly need your love and support six months, a year, or more after the traumatic event. Remember, just when the adults seem to be getting past the worst of their grief, that's when the youngest of the children will begin relapsing into the worst of theirs. Be there; be ready.

You should get ready to minister now. I had to admit I needed more training, more help to minister to children and families who were grieving. I enrolled in grief care classes offered through a local church, and I completed the course. What I learned there became precious tools many times over in my ministry. We go to trainings for a lot of things—recruiting, puppetry, new curriculums. Shouldn't we be training for how to handle times of crisis, too? You will face this, so you should be prepared. Find out what is offered in your area, your church, your denomination, books, and even college and online courses.

Make sure the child knows that what happened is not their fault. Children often blame themselves for their parents' divorce or even a pet's death. They need to hear from you and other adults they trust that what happened was not their fault. The parents and others around them will be looking to blame also. They will blame each other, blame other people, and probably also blame themselves. That huge load of shame makes the grief all that much worse. Blame will not help ease the pain of a loss. Sometimes a million reasons wouldn't make it all better either. They need to hear that God still loves them so much—that God still knows best—that even when we cannot understand, we can trust God's heart.

Tell the kids the truth. We do not like to scare kids by telling them that someone has died, so we tend to gloss over it, say strange things, or remove them as far from the grieving process as possible. The problem is that children are not stupid. They know partially what is going on and that you're hiding things from them, so they will not trust you. If they think you're making up stories, they may not believe you when you talk about the Bible and God's message of salvation either. If a child asks me, "Did my grandma die? Is she coming back? Is she scared down under the ground?" I will answer, "Yes, she did die. No, she is not coming back right now. We miss her so much. And they did put her body in a box in the ground, but you know, that is just her body. She's not really down there. That was just what was left when the real her, the part that thinks and knows—her soul—went to be with Jesus in heaven. You will see her again someday. It's okay to miss her and be sad, though. I miss her, too. Sometimes I don't understand why people die or why bad things happen, but I've learned that I can always trust God, because He loves me, and He loves you. I know He will carry you through this tough time. I am here, and your parents are here. We love you, too."

If they ask a tough question, try to answer it as plainly, honestly, and non-scary as you can. Make sure you include their parents in the conversations, too. Keep an open dialogue without shaming or lying to the child. In the months and years to come that child will continue to come to you, the Bible, and their parents with those questions, to pray through them together.

WHAT IF A CHILD TELLS YOU OR ONE OF YOUR LEADERS THAT THEY ARE BEING BULLIED OR ABUSED?

First, as you should already know, any time a child tells you or any of your leaders that they are being abused in any way you are morally and legally bound to report it immediately to your supervisor. Anyone who works with, teaches, ministers to, or volunteers with children is already legally a "mandatory reporter", meaning you could get in a lot of legal trouble if it ever came to light that a child told you about abuse and you did not report it. No excuses.

You should tell your supervisor or lead pastor as soon as the service ends. They should at that point inform the police or social services. You cannot afford to ignore a child's cry for help. That very same day, I highly recommend you write down thoroughly everything that was said, when, and to whom. This is an incident report and should be kept on file.

What if the child tells you they are being bullied? Did you know that bullying happens in the church, too? I've got some strong opinions on it, and you should too. I understand that what I am about to say is going to irritate some people and will go against mainstream "anti-bullying" teachings, but I feel it needs to be said. The way we're teaching parents, kids, families, and our kids' leaders to respond to bullying in the church is not biblical and it is not working. It's time to have some better conversations about bullying.

Bullying is something I understand well from personal experience. As the smallest kid in my class, with my "Coke-bottle" glasses, and poor out-of-date clothing (parents were pastoring a small country church), I was often the object of teasing, name calling, and pranks. It didn't help that I was a Christian or that I was usually ahead on my work. I'm sure that my reaction wasn't the best every time either. I'm a scrapper, so, small as I was, I usually lost my temper and responded with one whopping fight, which couldn't have helped my Christian witness. But I got through it, with the help of my church, my awesome Christian friends, and especially my parents. These days, I like going into public schools to talk about bullying and how we should respond to it. As a children's pastor, I see the results of children being bullied and it breaks my heart. I've given a lot of thought as to what my parents did right when one of their children was being bullied and what I see going so wrong in other situations. How should parents respond when their child tells them they are being bullied? How should a schoolteacher react? A children's church leader? It may not be what you think.

Here are awful ways that adults respond when a child reports being bullied.

Child: This kid is so mean to me. Every day they keep hitting me and calling me names. I keep crying, and I don't want to go to school anymore.

Adult: Well, that's a part of growing up. (haha) That happened to me in school, too. Yup, it happens.

What the child heard: "The abuse that is happening to you is not really a big deal. Everyone goes through it. It doesn't bother me that you're being abused, and it shouldn't bother you either. It will just go away. You being teased, hit, hurt, and rejected does not concern me much. It's going to keep happening, but you probably should not talk to me about it, because I don't want to hear it. In fact, I laugh because, like your abusers, I find your abuse kind of funny."

Adult: God said to turn the other cheek and forgive. So stop giving in to hate and get over it. Just forgive and forget.

What the child heard: God does not care that you are being hurt. You're wrong in this for feeling angry and hurt. You should have been instantly over it and never think of it again. God says you are supposed to take abuse, and if you ever speak up, or have feelings about it, you're wrong. It should be so easy to just get over it, because it was all so small anyway.

Adult: There are always two sides, and I didn't see what happened. Both of you say sorry to each other, hug, and make up. Next time, work it out between the two of you and don't bug me with it.

What the child heard: I don't totally trust you, and you may be lying. Also, you getting abused must be partially your fault. Both of you say sorry and immediately get over it. I will make you hug the person who hurts you. I will tell the other person that you told on them and then leave you unprotected at that person's mercy. Your problem was just a little kid problem, a little kid argument that does not mean much to me. You're irritating me, taking up my time, and I need to get this over with. I'm not a safe person to come to with this. Also, you are totally and completely on your own. It is you versus this person. No one is coming to help you or set this right. No one is there to protect you, defend you, or stop the abuse. You have to fend for yourself, but you still can't fight back or you'll be in trouble. All adults in your life, and even God, have left you to get tortured, abused, and beaten day after day. Later in life, this may lead to living with abusive marriages, job situations, and "friendships" because you believe you're not worth anything. Being a good Christian means being a total milk toast doormat.

So if these most frequent adult responses to bullying are not quite appropriate, then how should the parent, teacher, and church leader respond when a child tells you they are being bullied? For starters, let's call bullying what it is—abuse—emotional, physical, and mental abuse that is occurring on a regular basis in this child's life. Calling it "bullying" trivializes and downplays the abuse. This fosters a dismissive attitude of "kids will be kids!" Abuse of any kind should never be condoned or allowed to go on.

We need to look at the whole of Scripture. Yes, we're to turn the other cheek and forgive and show the love of Christ, but, you cannot dismiss the rest of the Bible. Paul, when he was about to be beaten for something he didn't do, invoked his rights as a Roman citizen (Acts 22). Paul also had a habit of calling people on the carpet for their bad behavior, both

Christians and non-Christians. When a slave ran away, pleading to Paul for help, Paul gets involved and pleads for the young man (book of Philemon). When Jesus is illegally arrested and abused, He never says, "Oh, that's okay. No problem." He forgives His abusers, yes. But He also calls them out on their bad behavior (John 18:23). He lets them know none of what they are doing is okay. Human nature is fallen and broken, and that's why we will always have bullies who will prey on the younger, the weaker, the quieter, and the different.

Part of our calling is to stand up for the weak. Isaiah 61, *"A broken reed He will not break."* Look around! Those broken ones are all around us. And what about the bullies? They also need a balance. They need grace and the love of Jesus, because they are broken too. They need to know it isn't right for them to be abused either. They also desperately need to be told they are worth saying "No" to, being given limits, and being given a different way to handle their feelings. If you really love a child who is acting like a bully, you will intervene before they end up wrecking their lives in selfishness, violence, and emptiness. Jesus loves the abused and the abuser. Change starts when someone steps into the situation.

THIS IS HOW THESE CONVERSATIONS COULD GO BETTER.

Child: This kid is so mean to me. Every day he keeps hitting me and calling me names. I keep crying, and I don't want to go to school anymore.

Adult: I'm so sorry to hear that. That should not be happening. It is not okay that you are getting hit. I care about you, and God cares about you. God would never be okay with you being hit and hurt. Tell me more. Why do you think this person is doing this? Who are they? Let's pray for them right now. We also need to tell your parents right away and your teacher/church leader. We'll work together to stop this from happening, because we want you to be safe. Thank you for telling me. This is not your fault. Nobody deserves

to be abused. You should always tell an adult when someone threatens you, destroys your property, teases you, or hits you. It is not okay for them to be doing that. We adults are not perfect, and sometimes we forget to listen well. So if one adult does not listen, then tell another adult, and another, and another until one of us listens to you. It's best for the person hitting you to get help too to stop what they are doing. You should not have to be afraid to go to school.

To sum it all up, you do not have to be perfect to minister to a family or a child in crisis. You just need to be there, to listen, and to point them to Jesus. Let them know, "We will face this together. You do not have to act out in anger or desperation. I'm here and you are not alone."

"Every child deserves a champion, an adult who will never give up on them, who understands the power of connection." - Rita Pierson

When you step up for a child in crisis, you are that champion. That's the way to show them Jesus.

CHAPTER 4
ALL OF HIS KIDS—SPECIAL NEEDS KIDS' MINISTRY IN YOUR CHURCH

"Thank you for taking a moment to talk with me," this mom said over the phone. On a busy Monday, packed with meetings, I was lucky to sandwich in a few minutes for phone calls before the day ended. But something in this mom's voice caught my attention. I grabbed my pen and paper in case she was about to bring up a problem, need, or complaint. To my surprise, she said, "I just wanted to thank your team for the service for my kids this past Sunday." "Um, you bet, you're welcome!" I managed. "We're always striving to make our services connect with kids and have an impact." After a moment of silence, the mother continued, "Well, you see, Pastor Trisha, my husband Neil is the worship pastor at _____ church downtown. Actually, I am a licensed worship pastor myself. My husband and I used to lead worship together there. And I miss it so much."

I waited with baited breath for her to tell me she quit ministry due to conflict issues or leadership struggles. But instead she said this. "We couldn't wait to start a family. But our boys, who were born a year apart, are both autistic, and pretty severe on the spectrum. We soon began to feel unwelcome at the church we had pretty much lived at all those

years before. I could no longer serve because I had to take care of the boys. And then came the day that the children's ministry could not accept them, and they made noises in main service. I loved our church. I lived for those services. Now, I have not been in any church service for over 3 years, because I have to stay home with the boys. I feel like we are pariahs, cast out of God's house, and it has been so hard (she started crying here). But last Sunday, I decided to try out one of your site churches that meets in a school. I thought that might be smaller/easier to quickly leave if things got bad. I called ahead and explained the whole situation to one of your staff, and she told me to come on ahead. (Inside I was doing a happy dance, because I knew that staff member has a huge heart for kids with special needs.) I was terrified that this would be a disaster, so I sat just outside the door for the entire service. But your team never called me once! They didn't make a big deal when the boys made noises and even tried to include them in what was going on! I just sat in my car after the service, put my head on the steering wheel, and wept. Even though I didn't get to be in worship or hear the sermon, it felt so good just to be inside a church building again on a Sunday morning and to not be treated like a burden or a freak or a failure. (I had tears running down my own face at this point.) I just wanted to say thank you, and I want to give it another go this Sunday. Whether it works out or not, I am grateful that at least your team is trying." You know how your perspective can change in just five minutes? That team deserved a lot of credit that week for ministering like Jesus and showing grace.

I realize that this is a hot button topic right now. Autism is on the rise like never before. It used to be a rare thing for a church to have a special needs child in their services. Part of this was partially due to the shame, stigma, and "hiding" that has traditionally come with special needs—either physical or mental. These days there are so many children in our ministries with special needs—Down syndrome, cystic fibrosis, deafness, autism (all across the spectrum), ADHD, children from abuse and neglect situations (they have special needs too!) and many, many more needs than could be listed here. Unfortunately, terrible views of disability have taken hold and have dug a root into our churches. There is much fear and guilt associated with disabilities, as if someone must have done something wrong, or not had enough faith, or as if certain challenges were "contagious" from close contact. One of the deepest fears our children's ministry leaders have is of making a mistake, doing something wrong, or of inadvertedly "not ministering correctly" to a child with special needs. The needs can seem overwhelming. But gone are the days that we can ignore special needs family ministries. You already have several in your ministry and in your church right now. Perhaps even more importantly, how many families of children with special

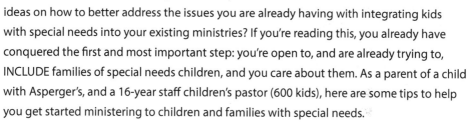

needs are not in your ministry, because they do not feel welcome at a church, any church? That question tears me up inside.

So what do you do if you and your church are considering ways to better include kids and families with special needs into your ministry? Need some ideas on how to better address the issues you are already having with integrating kids with special needs into your existing ministries? If you're reading this, you already have conquered the first and most important step: you're open to, and are already trying to, INCLUDE families of special needs children, and you care about them. As a parent of a child with Asperger's, and a 16-year staff children's pastor (600 kids), here are some tips to help you get started ministering to children and families with special needs.

Start small, but do start. If you stay afraid you will never step out. Make up your mind to take steps, even small ones, to reach out to families of children with special needs.

Set realistic expectations. If you build it they will come. The need is great, and so many families of special needs kids are looking for a place to go to church. I would highly suggest you let word of mouth do all your advertising at first. Be careful to manage those expectations and do not promise what you cannot deliver. A good idea would be to say, "We're just starting to reach out to families of special needs kids. We're in the process of expanding what we can offer and are looking for people with experience in working with special needs teaching/ministry to work with us." Remember: Promise low, deliver high. It's always better to exceed expectations.

Try having a sensory room. We created a sensory room for kids with severe needs (autism, etc.) who need a break. The schools gave us the sensory room items we needed. The sensory room is quiet, without any flashing lights, with many different textures to touch and feel—bean bag chairs, knobby toys, floor pads, etc. We know that all kids have good days and bad days. So we have the sensory room option open for tough days. Some kids who are sensitive to flashing lights or lots of worship noise may need some quieter time, and for us the sensory room has been helpful.

Special needs ministry can be non-integrated. We have been so extremely blessed with two older ladies, both of whom have raised autistic sons, who do our class for children with severe special needs—children who the parents do not want integrated. We work closely with parents to decide what works. Most kids with special needs are integrated, but this is about what works best for the individual child and their family. Some kids do better in a designated class, but this has to be taught by loving people who have experience working with special needs kids. You may not have this right away, but it may be something you want to work toward.

Make sure you can contact the parent at all times. Do not give out any medications or provide any medical treatments. This is a liability issue and still must be the sole responsibility of the parent. Do not make exceptions to this one. You must have a way to contact the parents at all times, even if you try not to use it unless you really need to. For safety reasons, do not accept any child in your ministry if you cannot quickly contact the parent (paging, cell, screen), especially a child with special needs. It is true that a church is not equipped to do what a school can do. That doesn't mean that we do not try to reach out and minister to these families. The question is: What is reasonable and full of grace in your ministry situation?

Look at each situation on a case-by-case basis. No two children are alike, and no two children have exactly the same severity of special needs. Two children with autism can be so far apart on the autism spectrum that their treatment plans may look nothing alike. Your first step is always to talk with the parents and try to understand the full situation and try to help the family understand your set-up. Don't promise what you cannot deliver. Listen a lot! I suggest writing down a plan for each child that you agree on with the parent. Evaluate it later to see how the ministry is going. Continually think of ideas for inclusion.

Get training for all of your leaders; offer them and track who attends. Before you throw up your hands and say, "We don't know anyone to do that kind of training!" hang on just a bit. We thought that too at first, but we were surprised by the great training that is out there and how eager people were to share it. Start looking with your local public schools. Do they have special education teachers willing to come out and do a training session for you? Look within your church. Are there teachers, nurses, or behavioral therapists you can ask to come in? Volunteers become afraid or overwhelmed when they do not have the training or the tools to address a child's special education needs.

The right training can help take away that fear and stigma, and make the class run so much more smoothly. We brought in a behavioral therapist who works with children with autism and Down syndrome, with their families at home, and in the classroom. We also brought in a public school special education teacher, and a parent of three autistic boys to do training, workshops, and Q&As with us. This was one of the best attended training events we've ever offered. When I travel doing workshops at churches, this workshop is the second most requested, right behind recruitment. Again, we're looking for tips toward including all kids in our 45-minute teaching session, not intensive interventions or medical treatments that we're not qualified to do. Let your leaders know that you're giving them the tools to be better children's leaders to their whole class, not counselors or medical practitioners. Remember, the parent is always the primary caregiver at all times.

The key here to successfully incorporating children with special needs into your kids' ministry is balance. I've seen churches turn all sound down, forbid faster songs, get rid of flashing lights, eliminate puppets and costumed characters, stop all black light productions. To me, this is going too far in the other direction. You're there for that hour to minister to all the children in attendance, of all learning styles. This takes a lot of wisdom and balance. Do we occasionally have rocking strobe light, black light roller blading costumed characters? Yes. It does happen. But because we intentionally plan our services pretty far ahead, I warn our teachers and parents of children with special needs when that element will be a part of our services. Then, the parent has the option to either sit with their child (which we love) or let them go to their classroom a bit early that day for a special activity until the rest of the class joins them. We keep our dynamic kids' worship services, and if it becomes too much for one of our kids, we have their classroom ready (which doesn't happen very often actually). We must be mindful and intentional when we craft our kids' services to reach out to that specific group of kids using several different approaches. Don't eliminate your illustrative methods, but have a back-up plan and communicate a lot with parents about what is going on.

Several churches I know, including ours, use "ministry buddies" for some of their children with special needs. This is an adult, a grandparent, or an older teenager (background checked and trained) who is one-on-one with that child for the whole service. This is someone for them to sit with, ask questions of, and get help from if needed. Again, the parent is the one to talk with about this option. We found that recruiting for this was not as tough as we thought it might be. Some people don't want to be up-front teachers or leaders, but they are amazing at being a friend to a child for an hour on Sunday. They have no idea what an impact for Jesus they make. One Sunday at our church, a mom came to church with her two severely disabled children, Caleb and Donovan, both with cerebral palsy and confined to wheelchairs since birth. She planned to walk them up and down the halls and try to listen to the sermon over the loud speaker. She was that desperate to hear from God. To her astonishment, two of our "dads" (volunteers who sit with special needs kids in the services), talked with her, introduced themselves, and checked her boys into kids' ministry. During the remainder of the service they just walked the halls pushing the boys, took them to our kids' worship service, prayed with them, and walked around some more. The "dads" may still not realize how huge their ministry that morning was or what an impact their kindness made for eternity. The mom told me she sat in the second row through worship, just soaking in the presence of God. She said both boys loved the kids' service and wanted to come back!

Start a parent support team. One side effect of opening up our kids' ministry to more and more children of different needs was that more families started attending our church! These families began having Bible studies together and taking time to pray with and encourage each other. Some of the fantastic by-products of these families of special needs meetings were:

- We found connections, ideas for our leaders' trainings.
- We were able to run ideas past these parents and really partner with them in the kids' ministry.
- They helped us with recruiting and finding "ministry buddies."
- We got to hear all the latest and best in special needs ministry.
- We had a voice in the community for family special needs ministry (which had us growing fast in that area).
- These families felt supported, connected, and understood.

What would Jesus do, if that child with ADHD came to His church on Sunday? I know Jesus would take that child in His arms and bless her, like He would all of the other kids and their parents. I know the challenges can be big and seem scary, but if we focus on getting started, if we focus on what we can do instead of what we can't do, I know we will be surprised at the miracles of ministry God will do through us. We don't have to be perfect. We just have to be willing to reach out. What small steps can we take right now, this week, to welcome special needs kids and their families into our ministries?

CHAPTER 5
THAT FIRST OUTREACH—
VBS, MUSICALS, AND MORE

"Great job on updating our kids' areas, Joshua," Pastor raved. "I took a walk through the pre-k areas this Sunday with a new family, and I have to say, I was nervous at first by some of the early designs, but those areas are coming along beautifully! It looks like we are still on track to be done by fall."

Joshua beamed. "Yeah, I'm so excited. A lot of parents were pointing and asking questions. People are so excited already. I see the space updates creating a lot of excitement and buzz! We're already starting to see some new families visiting to check out what's going on."

"That's wonderful!" said Pastor. "I did have one question for you though. Will the renovations be done by the time you do your VBS? If not, we need to have a back-up plan to work around the construction for that week."

"VBS? Oh, yeah, I forgot about that for the moment. At least that is a long way off—five whole months! I've helped the last children's pastor with our VBS programs several years in a row now, so that won't be too tough. What if we just don't do it this year due to construction?" Joshua was just offering ideas out loud.

"Not do our VBS?" Pastor half weezed and then coughed. His mouth had fallen open in shock, as if Joshua had just suggested erecting a Buddha in the foyer. "Joshua, we always have our VBS. You know that. We're known all over the community for our VBS each summer. What about the volunteers and families who live for VBS? No way! We must have our VBS. Don't worry, just get a team together and make it great. Think of this as a wonderful opportunity for you to show the families of our church how capable you are!"

"Ugh" thought Joshua. This wasn't sounding like too much fun. But Pastor seemed pretty determined. "No problem, Pastor. It'll be an amazing outreach, just you wait."

"That's great. I look forward to hearing your plans for it! You can tell us all about it at staff meeting next week, Joshua."

Joshua left pastor's office, thinking to himself, "Plans? Oh great. I'm going to have to get a VBS together and pull it off; but at least I have five months to do it. That's a lot of time, right? Just pick one, and do it. Sounds good. How hard could it be?"

When he got home, he sat down at his laptop on the couch to look at Vacation Bible School programs. That's it. He'd just pick one. His wife was folding laundry next to him. Hmm … "Jungle Jump," he thought out loud. "That would work fine for our VBS. I'll just get that one. It's popular this year."

"It sure is popular this year," his wife interrupted his personal monologue. "Christ Church is doing that one in July. Oh, and I think United Brethren and First Lutheran are doing that same VBS in June, too. "

"What?" Joshua was irritated. "I don't want to do the same one all the others are doing right next door. Well, that one is off the table. How about this one, Racing for Change. That one sounds like fun."

"It should sound like fun," his wife answered. "You and the last children's pastor did that VBS two years ago. Yes, everyone loved it, but you know how Pastor doesn't like repeating old VBSs."

"Arg!" Joshua griped. "Okay, here's a glitzy one! Grace Tails … oooh it comes with a video pack and all kinds of training materials and set ideas. This could work."

Rachel leaned in toward the laptop screen for a better look. "Joshua, you know that Pastor only left you a certain amount in the budget for VBS—the curriculum, the snacks, the prizes, and the sets. VBS is more than three times that amount for just the curriculum!"

Joshua snapped, "You have gotta be kidding me. This is ridiculous! At least I have five months to work on this." He put his head in his hands.

Rachel looked at him with sympathy. "Oh honey, five months is not long at all when you're talking about a VBS. We're really going to be crunched for time now. Also, this date you have here will not work. That's the annual men's ministries conference and they already have the church reserved. And the week before that won't work either, because that's when the three larger churches near us do theirs, and most of our families attend the other church's VBSs as well as ours.

"Wow. These detail people are so necessary and yet so annoying," Joshua thought. This was already taking a lot longer than he had hoped. "I really do not want to do our VBS when another church is doing theirs. So we'll just plan ours for a different weekend." Rachel hesitated before she responded. "Josh, every church in town is doing a VBS. They always do. Every week is booked by one of them. They've had their dates and themes set in stone for at least a year now."

A year? That just didn't seem possible. He thought, "How did this start going in the wrong direction? How did I go from 'easy fix to placate the pastor' to 'major undertaking for which I am already behind'? And why are we doing this again?"

If any of Pastor Joshua's dilemma sounds familiar, it's probably because you've worked on kids' and family outreaches yourself. In fact, the vast majority of U.S. Protestant churches will do at least one children's/family outreach this summer. If you have ever done a major kids' ministry outreach or are in the middle of one right now, you know the moment always does come, in the midst of all that hard work and planning, when you will ask yourself again, "Why did we get ourselves into this?" It is so necessary to have a clear cut vision, so that when the work gets tough, you'll remember that there are so many kids and families right where you live who have never heard the message of Jesus Christ yet. So why do we do this thing called outreach? We know we're called to go, called to grow, and called to share our faith. Our community needs us, and we need to be serving. According to Mark 16:15, which is known as the Great Commission for a reason (not the "Mild Suggestion"), Jesus' final command to us before leaving earth was, *"Go into all the world and tell them the good news."* It wasn't up for debate. It wasn't only to certain people. And we know that just looking around our neighborhoods, the need is huge. As long as people all around us don't know Jesus, then we have a big job to do.

What exactly is an outreach? Great question! What counts as a ministry outreach? By definition, a ministry outreach is a targeted effort by your team to present the message of Jesus Christ to those who are not yet living for/following Christ. A common mistake that we make sometimes is creating fun social events for our own church families and then labeling them outreaches. A bonding event for our own churched families is more correctly called a connecting event. There is absolutely nothing wrong with having connecting events, team building events, and family events. We do several of those every year. But an outreach always includes reaching out to unchurched people. An outreach could be a VBS, a musical, a sports camp, or a service opportunity (medical clinic, food drive, community clean-up) The goal of the event will change the way the event is planned and carried out.

How important is it that we even do outreach? I have actually heard this line of thinking more and more lately, *"Since parents are the key spiritual leaders in the home (true), the church should not be doing outreaches for children. Outreaches for children only are not very successful. So we won't do large events or outreaches anymore. Instead, we'll put our efforts towards equipping the parents who are in our church already. Our outreach will be solely through the adults we bring in to the main sanctuary."* Anyone who knows me, knows how strongly opposed I am to this way of thinking. Several of my key leaders and staff came to Christ in children's outreaches or camps, even when their parents did not come to Christ until years later (or not at all). Family ministry does not excuse us from the Great Commission. There's no excuse for failing to reach lost people. I've also heard some churches say, "Well, some churches do evangelism and some do missions, but we do discipleship." That's as ludicrous as saying, "I've decided for my fruit of the Spirit to have love, joy, and peace, and she is going to have gentleness and self control." We don't get to pick and choose God's directives. We have to balance outreach, service, discipleship, and more to be a healthy community of faith. Churches who do not place a high priority, in budget and volunteer power, on evangelism and outreach are already on their way to total decline whether they see it yet or not. Outreach is the very heartbeat of God, and therefore it should be our heartbeat as well. God's heart is broken for His kids in your area who do not yet know Him. Our job, and our privilege, is to set up that meeting!

What about the assertion that children's outreaches are not effective? The evidence simply does not support that statement. There are a lot of factors here that we need to consider. Are the parents in church? Are they living it at home? What follow-up is being done after the outreach? Did the child or the family come back to church and get connected? In book one, we talked about how so many homes are now "child-driven homes" and that the majority of families are looking for places that cater to their child's perceived needs and wants. Because of this cultural shift, your family and children's ministries can be your church's best and most effective team for outreach ministry! Families who would never willingly set foot in your church may be more than happy to send their children to your VBS or bring their whole family to your Harvest Fest. Many non-Christian families see nothing wrong with their children going to church activities because they are fun, safe, and teach "good moral values." The parent may attend with the child, because they believe they will be safe from hearing a powerful message, because it's "for kids." Your family talent night for Awana can become an outreach by inviting all unchurched parents to watch their child "perform" and then closing with a hard hitting message, worship, prayer, and cinching the whole thing with flawless follow-up. The need is huge. As long as so many do not know Jesus, we have a enormous job to do. Should you do outreach? Absolutely. Later in this chapter, we will talk more about how to do outreach well.

And when you do start planning your amazing outreach, the question may come up: Are we going to do a children's only outreach or a family outreach? I believe that all of your family/ children's ministry outreaches should be family outreaches, meaning that you should do everything in your power to bring in the whole family to whatever outreach you're doing. Have you noticed that all the top movies of the last few years were for families to see together? *(Toy Story, Shrek, Frozen)*. Parents seek out activities that they can do with their child and with a minimal amount of boredom and suffering for them. Smart moviemakers have recognized and capitalized on this. How can you make your outreach appeal to an entire family? Could you put your VBS in the evenings and ask parents to attend with their child? Can you advertise your Christmas musical as a family event? I always try to vision cast our kids' ministry events as family events for several reasons.

- This should lessen your recruitment burden by having parents watching their own kids. It frees up more of your leaders to teach, instead of being crowd control. However, you will still need a few leaders to sit with the kids who do not have an adult with them. I do not turn away kids who come to events without parents. We include them anyway with our designated leaders, but I still advertise it as a family event.

- Those parents may just as easily be reached by the simple message of Jesus Christ right along with their children. We have had whole families come to Christ every year at a children's outreach.

- You need the parents to see and experience what their children are doing, so they understand what their children will be raving about. And when you talk about what is coming up next and invite them to come, that parent will probably be the one driving them there!

- You're much more likely to get accurate follow-up information from a parent than from a child. Too many children cannot tell you their address or their parent's email address!

Some of my fellow children's pastors serve in areas of the country where they are not getting much as far as parent participation. The children are bussed in, or the church is doing street ministry and going to the children. They're always trying to minister to the whole family, but if just the children show up, they minister with everything they have to the ones who are there. They're seeing lives transformed every week, and they know they are making a difference for the kingdom. So aim for families, then minister wholeheartedly to the ones who show up, regardless of age.

Are you planning your next event at your church? Here are some questions you need to ask and answer in detail long before the event.

Why are we doing this event? Though this may sound like a silly question, I run into churches all the time who cannot answer this question for particular events. They'll say, "Well, we've been doing _____ for so many years. I don't remember exactly who started it." Do not continue to do an event "because we always have." Another bad reason to do an outreach is, "We just thought we should do something to pass the time in the summer." You already know how I feel about killing time and ministry.

Why is our church doing the event we're planning? _____
_____
_____
_____

Who has the burning passion for this project right now? If you cannot find anyone who has a huge passion and vision for this event anymore, it's probably time to stop doing that particular event.
_____
_____

What need does this event meet in our community and/or our church? If this event does not meet an identifiable need, it probably needs to be retired.
_____
_____

Who is our target audience? Are you hoping for an audience made up of non-Christians, church people, parents, professionals, college students? Identifying your target audience should guide and shape everything you do and how you get your message across. This is how you set your goals for the events and decide if it was a success or not. Who are you trying to reach with this event? _____
_____

Is our event a family connecting event, or an outreach? It is possible to be both, but if it is truly an outreach, you must involve non-churched people. Most importantly, if this is an outreach, you need to have your follow-up plan in place long before the event. How would I describe our event (connecting, team building, awards, outreach or combination)?

_____

_____

What is our plan for bringing these kids and families back and plugging them in to our church? This is the downfall of too many church events—tons of planning, sweat, hard work, tears, budget dollars, but all those new people never come back to visit your church. The number of people who come back and eventually begin to attend your church is called retention.

How important is retention? It should be your top priority and your main goal of the outreach. A child or a parent who accepts Christ as Savior at your outreach has a much better chance of keeping their faith and growing in their walk if they get plugged into a home church. I've even heard it said that when we tell people about Jesus, but do not follow up and plug them in, it's like we're inoculating them against Jesus. They hear the message over and over and over without any tangible life change, so they start to believe they are somehow right with God. Scary! Your church should be growing through the outreaches you're doing.

I've advised churches not to do certain outreaches if they don't have a clear plan for follow-up. I suggest having every person register at the door with name, address, and email. Then, intentionally block off time with you and your team right after the event (despite your exhaustion) to follow up on each and every visitor. Finishing the event itself is not "End Zone" so to speak. When you finish your event your team "brought the ball really far down the field," but the game's not over yet. Now your follow-up will either kick you that field goal or fumble.

OVERVIEW OF A FEW OUTREACH OPTIONS

Having covered why we do outreach and what questions to ask before you start, how would you like a few ideas on what kind of kids'/family outreaches are out there? Let's take a look at the most popular options, and I'll give you the pros and cons of each. It's best to do your research and make a well-planned, informed decision about which method of outreach best serves the culture, vision of your city, and your church.

VACATION BIBLE SCHOOL (VBS)

This is the oldest and most popular of outreaches. Typically this is a 3-5 day/night themed event, with activities for children and/or families with crafts, contests, games, and drama. What is great about VBS? Well, for starters …

More Variety. Because it's been around the longest and is the most popular, it has the most curriculums out there to choose from. Check out Group Publishing, LifeWay Kids, ChristianBook.com, and eChurchDepot.com to get started seeing what's out there.

Brand Recognition. Another great plus of Vacation Bible Schools is brand recognition. Depending on where you live, most people in your area already know what a VBS is. Families, both churched and unchurched, will be looking for VBSs to send their children to this summer. Some look for VBSs just for something for their kids to do, others for free childcare, and still others really value the spiritual experience. Many of these parents remember their VBSs from childhood! You probably will waste very little time trying to explain and vision cast what a Vacation Bible School is, although you may have to vision cast any new direction for your own individualized VBS.

Easier Recruiting. Almost everyone knows what you're talking about when you recruit for VBS. It's known to be a lot of fun and a tradition for many of your leaders. VBS is also great for your new Christians and those who like to serve one time. All the people who are not teaching for you week-to-week can jump in! It should be an easier ask to get people to commit to one week that's a lot of fun. This is a good thing, because you're going to need a LOT of help.

Simple Skill Set, Limited Supplies Needed. Most VBSs do not need special equipment or skills. VBS curriculum is typically written to work in all sizes of churches. This means, you should not need a lot of expensive sets, tech equipment, or unicyclists to pull it off well. The authors intentionally work to make use of what they think you will already have on hand, ie. cotton balls, paper, cloth, etc. Churches who do not have a full-time children's pastor on staff or high tech strobe light equipment should still be able to have a great Vacation Bible School experience.

KID'S/FAMILY TALENT SHOW, CONNECTING NIGHT, AWARDS NIGHT

Anytime you incorporate a reward for kids or a chance for the kids to participate, you create massive appeal and community pull. Never underestimate the impact. Remember what I said about child-driven homes? Yeah, whenever you have kids on the stage doing anything at all—singing, dancing, holding up signs, standing in a costume—every one of that child's aunts, grandmas, uncles, cousins, roommates, babysitters, and friends will be there, jockeying for position in the front row. This can be a great kickoff for your church's upcoming kids' programs—the fall kids' programs, an Awana launch, a new curriculum launch. Want to turn your next connecting event into an outreach? Have your kids' choir do a song at the awards, invite all of the parents to see their child promoted, and advertise well. Then make sure you follow up on each and every visiting parent, relative, and friend. Remember also, that if a child is getting to show off their break dancing for a talent night, they will probably bring a lot of their friends to watch. Be ready to reach those people on a special outreach night!

SERVING OUTREACH

This involves getting a team of loving, willing people together and going out into your community to share the love of Jesus through serving. You can help at the food pantries, rake leaves for the elderly, clean graffiti off of school walls, and so much more. No matter where you live, there are huge opportunities to help. You just have to find them. I don't believe that Christianity that stays within the walls of the church is real Christianity at all. Scripture tells us to help the poor, the broken, the widows, orphans, and the abandoned. Your own kids, families, and teams will grow so much in their compassion and in their ministry by doing serving outreaches. You will surprise your community, and remind them you are still there (out of sight out of mind)! You'll show unchurched people that you care about them and their families, like Jesus did, not just collecting offerings and preaching. Take special precautions to keep safety measures in place for your minors who go out for service ministry. You will also have to work hard to tie in the connection between the service and your church. (You want these people to get planted in a church.) Follow-up can be a lot harder after a serving outreach; in fact, one of the main complaints that communities raise is, "They swooped in, cleaned for an hour, and we never saw them again." A one-hit-wonder is nice, but it won't plug people in to your church long term. Have your plan in place to share the Gospel along with your service, and have a plan to connect the people you help with a church for a more lasting relationship.

KIDS' CRUSADE, BLAST, KIDS' SHOW, CONCERT, MUSICAL

The kids' crusade first became popular in the 1970s and 80s, along with Billy Graham's famous crusades. Whereas a VBS has a classroom feel, a kids' crusade is more of a fun, child-targeted church service. However, should you do an event like this, I highly recommend you change the name. "Crusade" has a very negative connotation these days. I call ours Kidzshow. Why would you want to choose a big kids' musical, play, or kids' church service for your outreach?

It has the potential to be a "wow" of memories. You can put all of your best on that stage and make an impression. Make them say "Wow!" and they'll listen to whatever else you have to say. Make it memorable! We've done a T-shirt canon, black light puppet disco-thon, and a trampoline dance. Creativity is king here!

The musical or kidzshow sometimes better incorporates parents and families. If you advertise this program as a free family event, you may get more parents to attend with their kids versus a traditional VBS. Having these families getting used to coming to your property is a benefit as well.

- An evening kids' program offers a chance for altar and worship experiences that will make a much more lasting impact. Lives are changed during worship, prayer, and altar times. VBS does not always offer any altar or prayer times.

- The teams that you train for this outreach—drama, worship, puppetry, altar teams—will be more experienced now. They'll be ready to jump in and bring your weekly programs to a whole new level. When we work this hard on our Kidzshows, our weekend quality afterwards goes sky high with such a highly trained, enthusiastic team.

- There will be families and kids who'll come back to your church, simply because they are hoping to get to do the things they see your team do on stage—sing, dance, act, lead. I always capitalize on this by announcing at the end of the event that we will be holding open enrollment for our weekend kids' ministry teams the second Saturday after the event, and that we're looking for kids who would like to sing, act, or lead on a ministry team. We always have families join the church after an event like this, because they want their child and their family to be a part of a quality ministry that's making a difference and that lets their child step out in their giftings.

• This kind of event should flow into your every weekend services. You can say something like, "Hey, if you liked what you experienced here tonight, please come join us this next weekend for our kids' church services. The same kids' worship team will be there, and your new puppet friends will be back this Sunday!" You should always aim to tie in your event to your every weekend ministry.

Cons of the kids' musical :

    • Need a new name (not kids' crusade).

    • There is potential cost of hiring an evangelist or special speaker if you don't feel comfortable doing this yourself.

    • You could possibly having to write some of your own material if you cannot find one that will fit your church.

    • "Kidzshow" may be harder to explain and vision cast than the better known VBS.

Full Disclosure: I personally have always written my own kids' outreaches called "KidzShows" (for the last 17 years) with dance, drama, and contests. I make them a family event. I usually don't do a Vacation Bible School, because our Kidzshow works really well for our church and our culture. Last week, though, I helped a friend's children's pastor with her church's VBS, and it was wonderful! So find out what works for your church, in your community, in this moment in time. Perhaps, you want to do an outreach not suggested here, and that's great! Be creative! Just do your homework and do your outreach well.

Beware of Common Pitfalls of the Children's/Family Outreach Event!

PITFALL 1: VERY GENERIC CURRICULUM

Some, but not all, of the curriculums I have reviewed over the years have been pretty bland and generic. This is because the authors are trying to make the VBS work for any church— all different sizes, cultures, and doctrines. They're trying to appeal to churched and unchurched kids, Christians and non-Christians, experienced leaders and new volunteers, kids ages 3-12 (which is a wide age span), evangelicals, Protestants, Catholics, and more.

The result can be very "non-offensive" but also pretty bland. For us, this meant extra work on our part, writing in illustrative elements and our own doctrinal distinctive to give it "flavor" and that "wow" factor. Some churches don't have the skill set or are uncomfortable with spicing up their VBS for more impact. The biggest complaint I hear is, "There's not enough Scripture used in this VBS. It's all just character lessons." So, make sure you look at it carefully, and decide how much extra work, if any, it needs, and how much you and your team can realistically put in.

PITFALL 2: POOR RETENTION
The major downfall of the traditional VBS and other kids' ministry events is often the terrible retention of new families (mostly from poor planning, lack of advertising, and no follow-up plan). Many families send their children to all of the VBSs in town all summer (10 weeks of them back to back!) simply for the free childcare. There is no intention on the part of these parents of sending the child to your church on a regular basis after the event ends. Since VBS has been viewed as childcare for so many years now, you will have to vision cast and work hard to forge a relationship with the children and families that can last into fall. Ask yourself, "What can we do to have these guests come back and visit our church and get plugged in as soon as possible?" On the flipside, if you don't ever see that child again, I still believe there is value in sharing the love of God with a child and pointing them to Him. How can you make your VBS a "wow" and stand out from all of the others going on in your area?

PITFALL 3: EXPENSE HIGHER THAN EXPECTED
Too many churches are not budgeting enough money toward family outreach. The curriculum costs can be relatively high, and let's not forget to include money for prizes, snacks, sets, costumes, game supplies, and advertising. Anything of quality is going to cost you. Set aside the budget you need to do your outreach well, and make it effective. Kids and parents can spot sloppy and thrown together; it will not bring them back.

PITFALL 4: HIGH VOLUNTEER NEED
You're going to need a lot of volunteers to pull off any family ministry event. You need check-in people, security, snack/food people, set-up and take-down teams, set and costume people, sound personnel, game coordinators, age group leaders, and drama team members. Make a comprehensive list of all the people you think you're going to need to make this event a success. Then, start making those specific asks, to fill specific positions far ahead of time. You'll need to meet with these teams often to plan, brainstorm, and problem solve.

PITFALL 5: MASSIVE TIME AND WORKLOAD COMMITMENT

Is the payoff worth it? No matter how you slice it, any major children's/family outreach is an enormous commitment of staff/volunteer hours, time, sweat, resources, energy, budget, and tears. Every year, the day before the event you'll think, "I can't do this. This is going to flop. I'm never ever doing one of these again." But the day after the event, you may change your mind if you "won" and met goals that couldn't happen any other way. Yes, there is a massive church-wide commitment to any family outreach event, so reassure yourself that the payoff is worth the use of all those resources.

Note: If a certain event or outreach does not have an identifiable leader who cares passionately for it (owns it, heads it up), if it is no longer serving the vision and direction of the church, and if it no longer is meeting or exceeding the goals you have set out for that event, you need to have the courage to let it go. There is nothing wrong with pulling the plug on a massive drain that is not giving you a payoff. We're stewards of the resources God has given us. Churches are notorious for attempting to put on too many shoddy events back to back. Better to do a few events with excellence and impact than to do several mediocre events just to say we did something.

PITFALL 6: NOT MUCH OF A FAMILY CONNECTION/COMPONENT

The traditional VBS or kids' outreach service, awards, or connecting event usually doesn't have a built-in family connection component. So you'll have to incorporate the family ministry elements into everything you do. There are ideas in this chapter on making your event a family ministry event, but whatever you do, work to connect your event to the whole family!

The Winning Checklist for Any Children's/Family Outreach

Start early … the earlier the better. Most great outreaches start planning, working, and meeting a year in advance. The very best time to start your planning and meetings with your teams is immediately after the last one ends, while it's still fresh in everyone's minds. **Take a lot of notes.** You'd be surprised what may slip your mind as soon as the event is over.

Rehearse and prepare or don't do it. Set the highest standards right from the outset. Destroy the outdated stereotypes by making your event stand out.

Showcase a lot of kids, not just the chosen few. The more children you can include in some way the better, even if it's not on the stage. Sign them up for offering, choir, handing out bulletins, and reciting verses.

Get prepared for the "mama drama." Nothing brings out the worst in people like their child not getting a certain part. Head this off from the get-go. See the chapter on conflict resolution.

Specific tips for kids' ministry outreach drama

Don't debate. Do not put your decisions up for debate or discussion. Let everyone know from the very beginning that we will do our best to choose the right person for the right part. All parts given are final, unless there is an illness or poor attendance at rehearsals. Do not argue with people over the decisions and placements, especially not publically. If you or your team's decisions during the planning of an outreach offend anyone, they should meet with you alone and in person. Try to let them know in love that you care about them and their child, and you hope they understand that this is a ministry, not a talent show. Do your best to win them over to your team, but do not give in to tears, anger, or bargaining. You are doing this outreach to reach lost people, not to make anyone a star (except Jesus). Stick by your team's decisions. Listen, but don't leave it up for argument or debate.

Have multiple judges and directors. I would urge you to not leave the decisions of who is in what part/role/solo entirely up to you. That makes you the major and only target of the frustration over unexpected decisions. I always work with a team of judges—ones I know I can trust, ones who understand quality and have a heart for the ministry and the lost. I keep my team small—3 or 4 of us at most. I reserve the final call in the case of a tie. When we do an outreach drama, Christmas play, or musical, we have children audition on a certain day and sign up online for a certain time slot. We have standardized sheets we use to take notes (because you will not remember everything later). We do allow rain checks for certain circumstances, but we do not advertise this in any way (case by case basis).

After the auditions and any last rain check auditions, the judges gather all of their notes and meet alone in a room to choose who will be in each role, complete with understudies. Sometimes, if enough kids try out, we double cast to include more kids (and then do 2 or 3 showings!) Double casting does add a whole lot of work, but it also adds more families that will be attending, and you then have built-in understudies! That means more families you can pull from to help in other ways with the production.

After you finish making your decisions, which may take time and a lot of prayer, do not post these in a public place. We used to post the outreach drama decisions on a certain wall of our church. After awhile it became known as the "wailing wall" as middle school girls sobbed at not getting a certain solo. Now we send out audition decisions entirely over private email. There will certainly be some disappointment, but it looks better if your team all came to the same conclusion. You do not want to make it look like you, and only you, were picking on their kid or showing favoritism. Working as a team protects you, and it has proven invaluable to me, in that my team sees so much that I do not! It is so much better with a team.

Ask for all complaints to be in writing! If someone is angry that their child did not get the drum solo, I would suggest gently and kindly asking them to write it all out for you. I tell them that I understand them being frustrated and would like to take a look at their story on paper. Those who have taken the time to write it out for me have helped me see into their child's heart, and that has helped me find ways to include that child and their family in more ministry. They liked the fact that I was actually taking the time to listen and read and respond in love. This forged some great relationships through the years. Other parents told me, "As I was writing it out, I suddenly realized that this is an outreach and I shouldn't be so upset about all this. How can we help?" If nothing else, you have a written record of the complaint to refer back to. Remember, you're doing this ministry to help the kids grow in their gifts and to reach lost people with the love of Jesus in a powerful way. You cannot make everyone happy along the way. Love people, but keep moving toward the goal.

Above all, use outreaches as a teaching opportunity to instill a love for serving God and others in your kids. I tell our young teams every week at rehearsal, "This is not about making us look good; this is about making Jesus look good. We do our best so that people will be drawn to Jesus. Your attitude trumps and is more important than your talent! I would rather have five of you up there so in love with Jesus and people, even if you cannot sing or act or dance at all, than to have 200 of the best actors, dancers, and singers in the world, who get up there to share with a nasty selfish attitude." They can almost recite this speech back to me now. By watching them minister, I know they get it. Teach serving, not a concert of popularity and showing off.

Do your best to work cross teams. Kids and family outreaches can never be fully carried out without help from other teams in your church. You're going to need help from sound/tech, perhaps your music pastor, worship pastor, or your drama director. Nothing we do is done in a bubble. It's easy to get laser focused on what our own ministry is doing and forget that there are so many other very important ministries going on in our church at the very same time. We assume each other area knows all about our event and cares about it as passionately as we do. When another area drops the ball, or we are not communicating as we should, it can be too easy to get a martyr complex and start feeling and expressing to others, "I'm the only one in this church who cares about the kids!" I would plead with you and your teams that as much as it depends on you, that you would strive to work as a team and be at peace with the other departments of the church. This will require a lot of over-communicating on your part, long before the event, thoroughly following up with heads of departments, a lot of patience, and at times communicating in various ways—email, letters, in person, voicemail, and even in a meeting with your lead pastor.

You will have to learn the delicate balance between kindness and persistence, forgiveness and confrontation, their needs and your area's needs. You really can be loving and patient, and still be passionate and persistent about that ministry. Do your best not to burn any bridges while trying to launch your event. An event is over in days, but the fallout of staff conflict can go on for years. If you know things are going sour, do not ignore the tension. Sit down and attempt to talk it out. If that fails, go in with your leader and that staff person. Above all, keep praying, praying, praying. This could be a great opportunity to forge a dynamic working relationship across teams that will last long after this outreach is done. God may be using these connections to take your every week ministry to another level! And if that other staff person is still not thrilled about a kids' event? Love them anyway. Pray that God will change their heart. But, you keep your eyes on the goal.

Be prepared to pay the toll. Jesus said, *"Count the cost."* It's best to go into an outreach knowing that this is going to be a huge job. It won't be easy. There will be several times you will not feel you have enough help. You'll feel that it will flop (especially the week before). Nothing great in life comes for free. An effective kids' and family outreach will come at a

heavy cost—to your energy, your time in general, your talents, time with your family, and your emotions. Know, going into your outreach, that this is going to be tough but worth it. With God's help, you will reach your goals!

Have your follow-up and retention plan in place and stick to it. Will you have everyone register at the door? Electronically or on paper? Who exactly will be going through the names and listing each and every visitor with emails and phone numbers? Which exact days and times will you and your team be doing follow-up? Will you use email, letters, phone calls, or a combination? Will you split the follow-up equally between the people on the team? Make sure you check back with your leaders and make sure they connected with everyone you assigned. I suggest having your follow-up letter from you ready to go before the event.

Put it in the evenings. More and more parents both have to work. Anything in the evening automatically is viewed as having more importance.

Work hard to get the whole family there. (See what we said under the "pitfalls" section on including the family.)

Adapt the curriculum (without breaking copyright!) for your church and your families' culture. How can you best get this group's attention?

Connect your VBS to what your church is doing as a whole. This increases your retention by leaps and bounds. Do the kids adore a certain puppet or costumed character at your event? Bring that character back on a regular basis for kids' church. Was the ice cream social after your VBS a hit with families? Then do it again for back to school.

Step up the quality of your weekly kids' ministry now. No, not after the outreach— right now! Just as important as the outreach itself are the four weeks of regular church immediately after the outreach. You may be tired, but this is part of the outreach. It's not additional. When those families do come back to check out your church after an event, they usually give you one chance, so make it count. If you really want to grow, you will have to raise the bar. Be ready!

Last but not least, I am going to give you a timeline that has been very helpful at our church and at other churches I have worked with. Feel free to print this off for your team and check it off as you go along!

Sample Timeline for a

Dynamic and Effective Family/Children's Outreach

ONE YEAR BEFORE THE EVENT

- Choose your outreach, by what is best for your church, culture, and goals.

- Get the word out now. Get your event on the church calendar ASAP and go ahead and reserve any needed vehicles, speakers, and equipment.

- Have a planning meeting with your team. Again, the best time to plan your next outreach is right after the current one, while it's all still fresh! You need honest feedback from a variety of people. Now is the time to get tips and ideas for the next outreach. Please see the back of this book for my "After Action Report" that I have all of my leaders fill out within 7 days of completing our event. Those forms have been priceless in the planning of our next event.

- Set a schedule for regular planning meetings to work on the outreach. Don't wait until the last minute. Pace yourself and work on it year round. I have a different team for each different outreach (Christmas musical team is different from the people on my Harvest Fest Team or Egg Hunt Team). I sit on all of these teams, but I give these leaders a lot of room to lead and be creative. You cannot do it all; a team approach works best.

9 MONTHS BEFORE

- Select and confirm your team. Delegate such tasks, such as advertising, communication, food service, cast check-in and checkout. I love having written job descriptions for each role. Let your team know exactly what you need them to do and by when.

- Stick to your schedule. Hold each other accountable to stay with the timeline. Keep everyone on task, reminded of the vision and progress.

- Make sure you are on track with your budget.

- Write a list of everything you're going to need as far as costumes and items. Start collecting those items right away and keep them in a safe place. Try to get things donated, check garage sales, and let people know what you need. You will save a lot of money collecting your materials early.

6 MONTHS BEFORE

- Put in your written requests with other church teams for needed rehearsal rooms, equipment, and needed staff for the event.

- Continue to do your regular team meetings.

- Continue to stay on top of your budget.

- Continue to collect your costumes and materials you need.

4 MONTHS BEFORE

- Hold auditions for key roles (if applicable). Assign parts and give out scripts.

- Keep your lead pastor/supervisor appraised of the progress of the event planning. I recommend sending your lead pastor/supervisor a one-page written update once or twice a month at this stage. Mention the event in staff meetings also.

- Vision cast to your congregation. Begin now to talk to your congregation about the outreach. Remember that people need to hear about it about 8 times, in many different ways, if you want to cut through all the communication noise they are hearing every day. Start communicating early and in as many ways as possible.

- Begin recruiting for all available positions (chart).

- Hold a parent meeting and make it mandatory for all families whose children will be serving in the outreach. I enclosed our sample parent pack/communication at the end of this book. Remember that conduct standards are crucial; explain this fully, and have parents sign the conduct form right there. Explain the vision and the heart of the ministry. Have a chart ready listing all the areas that you need helpers, and pass that chart around for parents to sign up right away.

- Begin your weekly rehearsals for your outreach/musical/dramas (if applicable).

3 MONTHS AHEAD

- Your leader meetings need to increase now to at least every other week.

- All rehearsals for your musicals or dramas are now in full swing. Keep enforcing high standards and attendance standards.

- Begin costume purchasing/development.

- Begin working on sets.

- Work on a written plan for tech, sound, and lighting. (See examples at the end of this book.)

- Meet with other teams to vision cast and confirm reservations. Send written reminders as well. Keep communicating the progress to your supervisor.

- Advertising needs to go into high gear. Advertising needs to start in earnest 4 months ahead—public schools, billboards, posters, handouts, overnight prints, postcards, coupons, and parades.

- Begin working on a retention plan!

1 MONTH BEFORE

- Rehearsals need to pick up at this point to twice a week.

- You should aim for at least 2 dress rehearsals with tech and costumes.

- Go to your church's prayer team and ask them to pray regularly for your outreach. Invite them to come in and have prayer with your team and your kids.

- Have someone taking notes at every meeting and rehearsal. You'll need to refer to them later.

- Step up your communication with your leader, all other teams, and the families of your church.

- Be prepared for the 4 weeks of kids' church that will happen right after the outreach.

- Finish all preparations for follow-up.

- Do one last all-out advertising push.

- Double-check that all volunteer positions are filled with emergency back-ups if necessary.

- Double-check that all materials and costumes are purchased and ready to go.

- Finish all sets before dress rehearsals.

THE DAY/NIGHT OF

You've done all the prep work at this point. Try to enjoy it now—smile, laugh, hug, pray. You need to be very present, encouraging, and flexible. When something goes wrong (not if) pull the focus back to the goal of the outreach. Something will always go wrong; keep going anyway, and make it a win regardless. Your job the night of is to keep encouraging and de-stressing your leaders, your team, and your kids. Meet and greet with new families as much as possible. Watch God work, and enjoy the fruits of all that hard preparation!

THE DAY AFTER

- Post outreach pictures and statistics. Collect written testimonies from your leaders and team.

- Expect post-outreach blues. Many children's ministry leaders are surprised to find that the day after an outreach they experience tears, sadness, and exhaustion. It's normal after such a big event that you've been planning and dreaming about for a whole year! Don't schedule major events during this time. You need to recover.

- Turn your phone off and get out of town for a day or two to recover.

- Send out After Action Report right away. (see end of the book)

- Schedule your debrief meeting within 7 days of the event.

- Celebrate! Make sure you have an amazing after party for all of your cast, crew, leaders, and their families. Read the testimonies, talk about all the wins, and look at the best pictures. Allow the members to share about what God did in their lives through the outreach. Ask them to commit to another year of ministry and making a difference.

- Schedule new leader trainings and welcome meetings for new families for the weeks immediately following your event. Be strategic about plugging these new families in!

Praise God you survived. Every time you complete an outreach or major project in ministry, you learn, grow, and get better. No outreach is perfect. Overcome and face your fear; God's grace shines brighter in our weakness. He can take what little we give and do the impossible. I like this quote: "Better to reach for the stars and come so close than to aim for the dirt and hit it head on." Jesus taught us to be "fishers of men." We are never more like Jesus than when we welcome His kids and even lay down our lives (and schedules and comfort) to bring them home. I wish you happy and effective fishing.

Love, Trisha

CHAPTER 6
YOUR CHURCH CONFLICT SURVIVAL GUIDE

Wall of Solutions

If you and I could walk together for a moment, in a graveyard of dead ministries, burned out, forgotten churches ... broken hearts and shattered dreams, those dead ministries would certainly make up a massive graveyard.

If we could see written on the headstones the reasons why these ministries ended or why the ministers left ministry, what do you think you would see there? I'm convinced that few of those headstones, or none at all, would say that the ministry or that heart for ministry died because of not enough money. As far as I know, no one wakes up one morning and

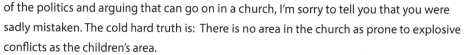

says, "Oh wait, I forgot, I hate ministering to people. I'll go be a plumber." And yet, as you may have already discovered, there is a very high turnover rate in both paid and volunteer ministers. And why? Not enough budget? Too many families to handle? I don't think so.

The number one reason that you will be tempted to quit your ministry is the fallout from poorly handled church conflict.

For those of you who chose to serve in the children's area, hoping that you could avoid a lot of the politics and arguing that can go on in a church, I'm sorry to tell you that you were sadly mistaken. The cold hard truth is: There is no area in the church as prone to explosive conflicts as the children's area.

Are you shaking your head right now? Are you thinking "No way. We wouldn't have arguing or hurt feelings happening in our kids' area!" Remember, that there is a lot of emotion involved when you are dealing with people's kids. Families may overlook a problem in the parking lot, or even put up with a service element they did not enjoy, but if their child gets hurt, or comes home crying, they will want answers … from you. Have you seen news specials lately about parents bullying teachers? That can spill over into the church. And of course, we're ministering to people who need Jesus (we all do!) We're ministering to people who are hurting and our own stressed out volunteer and staff teams. Unfortunately, we cannot eliminate conflict in the church. If our ministries are going to survive and thrive, we're going to have to get better at reducing and managing the disagreements that will occur. Unfortunately, many people in our congregations have no idea how to handle disagreements in a biblical manner. As leaders, we have to intentionally train people how God expects us to treat each other (Matthew 18). With that in mind as our end goal, here are a few very practical tips to surviving the conflicts that come our way. I really wish I had known some of these when I first went into ministry!

"Do not make their emergency, your emergency." This was the best, most eye-opening advice my boss ever gave me. Just because someone calls you, emails you saying something is an emergency, does not mean it is an emergency. That is giving that person too much power. Their emergency may take you away from important family time, much needed sleep, productive appointments, and other ministry. Just because someone demands a late night meeting or to see you immediately, does not mean you're obligated to do so. In fact, I routinely will wait a day or two, so they (and maybe I) will have time to calm down and prepare. Boundaries are so important for your family, for your health, and for relationship with Jesus Christ. When someone calls you during family time, prayer time, or personal time, let it go to voicemail. Then listen to the voicemail, but do not respond emotionally. Think first. Is this really an emergency? Can I schedule them for an appointment tomorrow or later this week? If their relative has just been in a car wreck, by all means go. If they're sobbing because their daughter did not get the solo in the Easter service, that issue can wait until tomorrow. You're not responsible to meet everyone's emotional needs. They have to deal with their own feelings. You can care and you can help … without being controlled. And if you set a precedent of always jumping and running whenever someone starts drama, you will always be jumping and running for every situation, eventually damaging your ministry, your health, and your family.

Never, ever, ever, ever, ever (times 2,135) work on a conflict or tough situation over email, Facebook, social media, or voicemail. I don't care what the excuse is. Trying to solve conflicts like that never leads to anything good. And it's not biblical. We're supposed to go to them and meet one-on-one with the goal of reconciliation. Email is notoriously misconstrued; you cannot hear someone's tone or inflection, or their heart. Don't leave room for misinterpretation. As tough as it sounds, bite the bullet and meet with them one-on-one to sincerely work it through. Do not engage in conflict in any way other than face-to-face. If someone expresses anger over social media or voicemail, do not respond in kind. Always, set up a face-to-face appointment (at the church or neutral ground is best).

Don't ever put anything in writing or voicemail that you don't want everyone to read or hear. A good friend of mine, a children's pastor, received an angry outrageous phone call from a parent one day while he was home sick. Without thinking, he called back and left a curt message on her voicemail. She responded by tearfully playing his voicemail message over and over in the parking lot of the church to anyone who would listen. He learned a painful lesson that day. If you aren't comfortable with anyone and everyone reading what you wrote or hearing what you said, then don't write it (or say it).

If your one-on-one meeting does not go well and there is no resolution, you're not off the hook to attack that person, or gossip, or get people on your side, even if that's what they're doing. Yes, Christians should know better but many of them don't. Lead by example. The goal is not winning or beating an opponent in a debate. You can win and still not win. The goal is love and redemption, even if you don't give them what they want. The next step in Matthew 18 is meeting with them with one witness. This should be your supervisor or lead pastor. And by the way, senior leaders usually hate being surprised. If you have a tough situation, talk to your leader as soon as possible. Better they hear it from you first! It is not gossip to keep your pastor in the loop, since your goal is reconciliation and they are over your area. That way, when that person goes over your head to your leader or you have to pull them into the conversation, your pastor will not be completely blindsided. They may also be able to give you some great input and advice. Then you're not facing it alone.

Do not delete emails or voicemails pertaining to the conflict. They may come in handy later with your supervisor.

As much as humanly possible, don't respond to angry letters, emails, or phone calls at all, when you are sick, overtired, grieving a loss, or in another situation that has you less than your best. Remember, you are not obligated to answer immediately. There will be moments in your ministry that you must deal with a situation when you're not at your best, but if you have any choice in the matter, delay that confrontation until you are rested and calm. This has been a big one for me to learn! Take care of you before you take care of the confrontation.

Cannot think of what to say in that moment? Clam up. "Silence cannot be misquoted." Silence is one of your best defenses. Don't say something that can be used against you. And they may keep talking themselves into a hole. It's okay, and wise, to say, "Hmm, I'm gonna take some time to think and pray about that, and I'll get back to you." Do not get pressured into making a final decision or a declarative statement too soon, simply because it's being demanded.

Do not respond to or acknowledge nasty anonymous emails and letters in any way. Anonymous confrontations are not biblical. Responding to them encourages that wrong behavior. Teach people right off the bat that misbehavior like that won't get them anywhere. Teach and model biblical behavior. You teach people how to treat you. Throw those mean letters out. Delete them and move on.

When people are nasty and mean, do not respond in kind. But there will be times that you need to let people know, in love, that they are out of line. What happens when you are challenged publically? If you ignore bad behavior, or retreat, or cower, or cry, you are only encouraging that negative talk and a continued acidic environment. Over time, I promise you that bad behavior does not just go away on its own; in fact, it tends to fester and escalate. You set that tone, so lead, and make it a positive gathering. It takes time, wisdom, and experience to learn to respond like Christ. He responded in love, while still unflinchingly calling people out on their sin.

Kindly confront when challenged publically, and here's how you can do that. When someone has made an unkind comment during a meeting or a public setting, I have answered in some of these ways: "I understand you feel that way. I care about you. I'm listening." "I have to ask you to refrain from name calling." "That was unkind. Let's keep this a productive time." "I hear you. But scripturally, that is a conversation for another time in private." "I totally understand there being a lot of emotion involved in this issue. We are a family of believers, and we love each other. But let's remember, even with our feelings and strong opinions, we are still bound to follow Scripture. What does God's Word say about this situation?" "Let's take a break here. We're not going to allow this to descend into a negative argument. Let's come back in 10 minutes, stretch, get a drink of water, and take a fresh, positive look at this." "Guys, remember, we're here to work together to solve the problem, not to blame. Who has an idea to fix this problem?"

Which leads us to …

In every situation, work to redirect blame to problem solving. Human nature seems to cause us to look at every problem, failure, and difficulty with the mindset of "Whose fault is this?" followed by, "How should they be punished?" This kind of thinking is destructive and only divides us. "Blame storming" sessions typically do nothing to solve the root problem. For example, I sat in one meeting recently watching the church staff argue at each other's throats for 36 minutes straight over who left the back door of the church unlocked after church the past Sunday. There was a lot of finger pointing, excuses, and defensiveness. But after all of this arguing, no one had come up with a single plan for making sure that the doors were all locked each evening. In a confrontation, it helps to bring a better resolution. Strive to redirect all parties involved from figuring out whom to blame and punish to work as a team to solve the problem. Remind them of the vision and overall goals you are working toward. The problem should seem much smaller in comparison to the massive, amazing work we are trying to do for God.

REMEMBER: BRAINSTORM NOT BLAME STORM

Sometimes, you will have to let some people go. This has been one of the hardest lessons for me to learn. I have one of those personalities that wants to make everyone happy and keep everyone my friend. In the church, we oftentimes have the misconception that we all have to be best friends with every single person. The truth is that we are called to love each other, no matter what. However, there will be those people, even in the church, who are not going to like you, no matter how you try, no matter what you do. A perfectionist like me struggles with this. Scripturally, you have to do what you can to make the peace, but there will be times that nothing you do seems to work. In those times, remember the non-negotiables. God is the One Who has called you, and you still have a big job to do for Him. You have to focus on the entirety of the ministry—all those families, and all those children. Do not allow yourself to be derailed and constantly distracted by one or two people's drama. Yes, we leave the 99 to search for the one. But when the one keeps biting you and all the other sheep, it's okay to let them go to (or send them to) another pen.

And what if someone has a very poisonous attitude and has no intention of stopping their behavior? What if you have tried to confront in love and have done everything you can think of to make things right? What if the attitudes and behavior of this person are hurting others in the church and poisoning the whole atmosphere? What if you have given chance after chance, and you are out of chances to give? Here is a great piece of advice from a lead pastor that I truly admire. I was talking to him about a volunteer teacher who was being repeatedly cruel to other teachers and parents despite a lot of coaching. She wouldn't stop until she made someone cry. I felt like if I asked her to step down, I would be a failure, and that I wouldn't be Christ-like. Here's my lead pastor's answer:

"Trish, I was very young when I took my first lead pastorate, fresh out of Bible College. I thought I had to keep everyone happy. I thought I couldn't ask anyone to leave. In that first church, there was a woman—the wife of a board member—who was especially difficult to deal with. With a

smile on her face, she would say the nastiest things to volunteers and parents. She didn't seem to be satisfied until she had made someone leave church crying. Several times that was my own wife who left church in tears. That woman single-handedly ran off so many new people and so many new families that I eventually lost count. After many meetings with her and her husband, and many broken promises on her part, I came to a crossroads. I knew that I needed to ask her and her husband to leave the church. But I was afraid. I was afraid of having to face them and ask them to leave, afraid to face the repercussions of that decision. I thought, "How many people will they take with them? What will they say to others? What will the board say?"

Out of my fear, I backed down, and instead chose to leave the church myself. I knew the church could not grow with her there, but instead of asking her to leave, I uprooted my family, and I left. Shortly after I left, she ran off 3 more pastors in less than 18 months. The final result? The last time I drove through that city, the doors to the church were boarded shut, and the building was for sale. One of my friends from that church asked me recently, "Why did you leave us, Pastor? Why did you let her run a growing church into the ground?" I didn't have a good answer, except that I was afraid. It is one of my biggest regrets. If I had asked her to leave, that church might still be growing today. Who might have come to Christ in that ministry? That's what haunts me. I let her win; everyone else lost. Have the courage to do what I couldn't do. Make the tough decisions with everyone in that ministry in mind, even if it means asking someone to step down or leave."

His words shook me to my core. I realized that instead of trying to focus on making every single person happy, I needed to focus on making God happy, and taking care of the ministry that God had called me to do—thinking of the WHOLE of that ministry. There are a lot of churches in this world and sometimes it's best for everyone involved to ask someone to join a new church family or take time off of a ministry position. Always as a last resort, I have had to have those tough conversations with difficult people, and even had to ask one or two to leave or to step down. I still do not ever enjoy these confrontations, but I understand it is sometimes necessary for the growth of the ministry.

Remember who called you. In my denomination, when someone is going for ordination, there is one question that is guaranteed to be asked and thoroughly discussed in detail during the licensing interviews. What is that question? "How do you know you are called to ministry?" Many candidates find this question offensive or are confused as to why the interviewers continue to insist on having an answer. This question is asked several times in different ways. Why? Because … when conflict happens in ministry—and it will—the only thing that will carry you through it is, "I know God called me, and He will get me through this." In the end, He is the One you are working to please. He is the One who loves you and approves of you.

Conflict in ministry is something we all face. It's something Jesus and all the apostles had to deal with. You may not have done anything wrong; in fact, your ministry may be doing things right but conflict is surfacing. Don't give up! Keep focused on doing the ministry God put you there to do, and God will go with you through this. Please be one of the ministers and ministries that make it for the long haul! The field is still white for the harvest and we need you.

CHAPTER 7
DISCIPLINE POLICIES
THAT WORK!

Several years back, my ministry team and I visited a larger church to speak for their Sunday morning kids' service. As excited as our team was, I couldn't help but notice that no one else at this church seemed excited for this kids' service at all. And no one was less excited for this kids' service than that week's kids' ministry team leader. You see, this church had a mandatory rotation of parents, and every parent had to take their turn.

This mom, a busy attorney, rushed in late and was already visibly irritated. She turned to me and said loudly enough for the kids to hear, "Well, in a minute they'll be all yours. Watch out, they don't listen to anyone. They're out of control. In fact, they're awful." That last part stung me like lemon juice on a paper cut. This kids' ministry obviously was suffering a few problems. In the next five minutes I knew exactly why. Pacing up and down the room, this sharp dressed lady began rolling up a newspaper saying, "You kids are so outta control. You are awful. If you start that junk like last week again, you are gonna get whacked." As my mouth fell open in horror, she began whacking the kids in the head that were talking in the back row. I turned to one of my teammates and mouthed the word, "lawsuit." The beginning few minutes were so boring and unorganized that our team kept finding ourselves misbehaving (talking, gesturing, writing on bulletins).

Not shockingly, when our part of the service finally started, we didn't have any discipline problems at all. We had a fantastic altar response time and really bonded with the kids while we were there. So, what was so different in the way each part of the service went?

Was it just because we were new and different? I don't think so. This is a question I get asked a lot: "What is an effective discipline policy for our kids' church/ classrooms?" It's so important, because just one or two children acting out can distract and ruin the lesson for all of the children, not to mention drive your volunteer leaders to distraction! You only have roughly an hour every week, so you need to make it count. How can you make sure you have their attention? How can you keep order?

First of all, let's stop blaming the kids. Remember what the kids' ministry leader snarled at me that day? She said, "They're all awful." But the truth is: "If you don't have a plan for them, they have a plan for you, and you won't like it!" The time and age we live in is unique, with the rise of ADHD, child-driven homes, under-equipped and understaffed schools, and at times no enforceable limits. But these same modern-age children are still craving rules, attention, and love. I highly recommend reading the books by Tim Elmore, especially *Artificial Maturity* and *Generation IY*. Dr. Elmore presents a compelling case that our kids are growing up too fast and too slow at the same time. We do not protect them fully from what will harm them (sex, drugs, death, violence, total independence), but we keep them from what would grow them in a good way (responsibility, hard work, leadership, sensible risk-taking and dealing with failure).

What a challenge and a great opportunity we have to introduce them to a God of non-negotiable rules, stability, and rewards! We do this best by modeling rules and order. The first step is for us in ministry to stop blaming the kids. You can't control another person; you can only control you and your programming. I've not found the myth of "they're all awful" to be true yet. In reality, if the majority of the children in your group are distracted, off topic, disengaged, and unenthusiastic, it's time to re-examine your programming and approach! Instead of blaming, yelling, and threatening the kids, let's craft an amazing experience they can't take their eyes off—a service they love being a part of!

So what are the best approaches to classroom discipline in a kids' ministry setting? With over 600 children each week spread out over 5 campuses, 31 classrooms with 200+ volunteers, it became absolutely essential for us to have orderly, fun services, so that everyone could hear the message and enjoy the experience. Here are the key points that helped our team develop our culture of classroom management.

Define the goal. Imagine if you were going on a trip to Disney World. Yay! But then when you arrived, you see you are in the Badlands of South Dakota. Beautiful? Absolutely. Definitely a good place to visit. But as far as the trip's objective goes, the trip was a failure, because you were supposed to end up at Disney World, and you didn't get there. To determine if your Sunday morning programs are winning, you and every single one of the people on your team, need to know all the way to your toes, what a winning Sunday really looks like. Is a win getting through the entire packet of curriculum for that day? Is a win getting more children to participate in prayer? Is it a win if the whole class prayed with a child who just lost a grandparent, even if you didn't finish the curriculum for that day? We said "yes" to that last one. One of our mottos here is, "People over Programming. Child over Curriculum." We have to continually train our team what a win looks like and what it does not. For us, it is not necessarily a win if the children stay silent and unmoving. It is not a win to just get through the material/service/hour. It is not a win to end early or have lots of games. For us, it's a win if more children participate this week in worship, prayer, fine arts, and group discussions. It's a win if they bring their friends. It's a win if they talk to us about serious life change—being more respectful to parents, committing to giving to others, refusing to lie anymore. It's a win when they "get it." I think it's a win when the parents have to stand in the back (and see what's going on) and wait a couple of minutes because our services are going so well. It's a win if parents notice the difference in their child and want to get involved. What is the win for your kids' ministry this Sunday? Do all of your leaders know the answer to that question? Your vision and goals will determine your discipline policy, not the other way around.

Plan, plan, plan ... way ahead. Most discipline problems in the classroom are the direct result of not enough planning. You know when you're winging it, and the kids do, too. As my mentor always said, "If you do not have a plan for them, they have a plan for you. And you are not going to like their plan." If you're not clearly in charge, with a well thought out plan, the kids will sense that and act accordingly. And by planning, I don't mean simply reading out of a book. As we covered in my first book, cold reading of curriculum is like opening a can of cold SpaghettiOs® and plopping it out on a plate. That is the lowest form of communication and will not keep anyone's attention (adult or child). Would you like sitting in silence listening to someone read for an hour? Our services should be crafted for maximum effectiveness; we have the most important message of all to give ... ever! It is a sin to make the message of Jesus and His love for us ... boring. When you're planning:

- Make sure there are opportunities for the children to participate (act out stories, build a project together). The more hands-on activities you can add the better.

- Change up your activities around every 5-10 minutes max. Anything over that timeframe without a change will likely be lost on them.

- You need to overplan. Do not be caught offguard by the adults getting out early. I usually plan at least 20 minutes of extra material, just in case. Worship and prayer are not extras; they are non-negotiables. But you can plan a craft, story, or game for any extra time.

- If an activity is not working, not connecting, and you can see the kids getting restless, then cut that story/activity short and go on to the next. No matter how awesome that element is, it is a waste if it's not connecting with the kids. If something is really connecting, and you know you have the kids' full attention, then feel free to extend that element a bit, or come back to it. Just make sure to leave them wanting more.

Have a written discipline policy and post it. As far as your official policy for classroom discipline goes, you need to be thinking objective as much as possible, not subjective. For example, you shouldn't be saying things to kids like, "You should know better" (many of them do not), "Stop acting up," "Cut all that out" (that is way too broad), or "You guys are being terrible today" (again, not very specific). When you have trouble explaining exactly which rule was broken and the steps you took to correct the behavior, it begins to look like you are singling out one child—picking on a certain kid—because you personally do not like them. It's always best to not make any of this personal.

Parents need to be your biggest partners and advocates; however, nothing brings out a parent's defensiveness and distrust than when they believe you are singling out their child. Objective policies, rewards, and consequences protect you. I also highly recommend that you post your classroom policies in several high traffic areas of your church. Send copies home for parents to sign. Have parents sign copies of your behavioral policy when they register their child. Put the policy on your kids' ministry bulletin and your website. Put it on the check-in desk, lost and found, visitor center, and by the bathrooms. How does this help you, your volunteers, and the parent? When a parent comes to pick up their child, I or my volunteer may have to explain to them that their child had a tough day. (We try not to do this very often.) I will explain the rule that was broken and exactly how we handled it, and all of the steps we took. "Jaden called a child a 'loser' within earshot of his teacher. Our leader asked him to not call names, because our rule number 3 is 'No mean talk.'" The first intervention is asking the child to stop. Point at the wall next to you and point out the rule clearly posted for the win! "Then it happened a second time 6 minutes later. We spoke with both boys and apparently this is an argument they were having at school this week that has spilled over into church. We used it as a teaching moment to talk about the love of Jesus and forgiveness. We asked Jaden to sit in the back by his teacher during worship, which is our second step in intervention. If it had happened again, we would have paged you. The rest of the kids' service went great; we just wanted you to know how we handled it. We cannot wait to see you and Jaden again next week. Please email or call me if you have any questions or insights for us." The clearly posted rules and carefully followed consequences show the parent you are not singling out their child, and that you care about ministering to every child. You have a plan in place and you're doing your best to follow it!

This works very well when you're talking with a child as well. I will point to the rule on the sign and say, "I know you want to run up and down the halls Kylie, but the answer is 'no.' See the rule? We do not want you to get hurt or lost. We don't allow anyone to run up and down the halls, especially during service. It wouldn't be fair to say 'no' to everyone else in the church, but to make an exception for only you. So let's be fair and follow the rules. I can trust you, right? Otherwise you'll have to sit in the back with Mr. Mike for today. Okay, glad to hear it. Thanks!" Printed rules carry more weight and are easier to enforce than rules that seem to be pulled out of the air.

Note: If a parent or child wants to know exactly what the consequences and discussions were for other children/families, do not get sidetracked by that. Don't start discussing other children, families, or situations. Keep pulling the conversation back to them and the situation at hand. "Yes, I did hear that Brandon was running too, and that situation is between him, his parents, and our team. I will not be talking about you with his parents and I will not be talking about him with you. Let's focus on you right now and making sure you understand the rules. Brandon's parents and I will take care of Brandon."

Keep it short and sweet. Too many churches make the mistake of putting their kids' church rules and policies in a gigantic binder, a binder that sits on a shelf collecting dust. They have long forgotten where their giant binder even is! Do you really think your parents or your leaders are going to read all the way through that binder or remember what is in it? You should have your kids' ministry policies and procedures on one paper, no more than front and back (2-sided). It's okay if this is a condensed version of your giant binder; I'm just telling you, that with the onslaught of info barraging your parents and leaders every day, they're not going to read and process your whole binder. So put what they really need to know onto two easy-to-read pages.

Please keep your discipline policy, especially the one you are posting, positive. When I'm visiting a church, and I see a classroom discipline policy that is one long list of rules and punishments, my first thoughts are, "Wow, they must really be having problems here," "This is not going to be fun," and "Maybe my kids should just stay with me." Your kids' ministry needs to be about having an experience in God's presence, connecting with great Christian friends and adult mentors, stepping out to serve, and having fun. If your program is well planned and well executed you shouldn't need a long list of threats posted everywhere. You only have one hour to make a difference. Don't waste the whole hour constantly correcting. See if you can tell the differences between these two posted classroom discipline policies.

"No swearing, no using God's Name in vain, no name calling, no disrespectfulness, no eye rolling, no spitting, no inappropriate noises, no poking, no hitting, no moving your chair, keep all four chair feet on the floor at all times, no crawling on the floor, no leaving, raise your hand if you want to speak, no interrupting, no fighting, no damaging property, no stealing, no bullying. If you do these things, we will tell your parents. You will be sent to 'big church.' We will tell the pastor on you, and you may be kicked out."

The above list actually went on for a lot longer than this. My problem with it and policies like it is that it's predominately negative, and it focuses on "no" instead of what you are there to do. Contrast the above policy with this one.

"We're so glad you're here today!
    A. Please pay attention at all times so that everyone can see and hear the whole program without distraction. This means no phones or electronics!
    B. For your safety, if you need to leave the room, please tell your teacher. Otherwise, stay in your seat and enjoy!
    C. Rough-housing, and horseplay is for other times and places. Hands to yourself in church, so no one is distracted.
    D. Church is an amazing place to meet with God and great friends. We do not do any mean talk in the house of God.
    E. Have fun! Participate! We hope you have a great time, leave having learned something new, and come back next week with some friends!

Anyone who is having a tough time paying attention and following the rules today will get one warning from their leader. On a second warning, they will need to sit with their leader in the back of the room while the service continues. On a third warning, we will meet together with your parents and figure out how we can help you have a better experience next week.

Let's have a great morning today at Kids' Rock Worship Center!

I really like the second policy better for several reasons.

- It focuses on the positive and reminds the parents, leaders, and children why we are really here today.

- It's short enough to post and refer back to as many times as needed.

- It covers most, if not all, of the major bases without trying to list each and every single infraction and penalty.

- It does not make anyone a bad guy or an enemy—not the parent, or the child, or the leader, or the pastor, or the church.

- The focus is not on punishment, alienation, or rejection. The focus is on ministry to that child for that hour.

- The first impression here is: "Something amazing and well planned is about to happen here today," "I don't want to miss this," and "Sounds fun!" This generates excitement for your kids' service instead of giving the child bad ideas or inciting rebellion. It left me really curious to see what they had planned for their kids' service, and they did not disappoint! Make it short, but make it sweet. Keep 'em coming back for more.

Train every leader and plan to refresh. It's interesting that the number one complaint I get when I'm doing consulting with a church from the kids' ministry volunteers is: "I did not get enough training for this volunteer position." Most children's pastors/directors would interject a scream here saying, "But I offer trainings and they do not show up!" Yes, I know. Please check out book one, *Your Children's Ministry From Scratch*, chapter 6, to see how to get those volunteers to your training! But it's still crucial that you offer training on topics such as classroom discipline, creative programming, dealing with children in crisis, and special needs training. Your leaders will be so much more confident if they have the tools to minister effectively. These topics just mentioned will need to be gone over many times and refreshed, even for your seasoned leaders.

Times change, techniques change, and your ministry dynamic may change (such as two brand new kids with ADHD). I suggest doing at least two trainings per year on classroom management topics. A great idea would be to put training on the above topics on DVD, or streaming video, on your kids' ministry website, so your volunteer leaders will have access to the training and tools to minister in their classroom and can train 24/7 as their schedule allows. We also have software that lets us know which of our volunteers have completed which volunteer trainings! Neat, huh? You cannot and should not be solely responsible for ministering to every child in that ministry. Your ministry can only grow as you empower and equip your children's leaders to do their ministry. As I tell my team, "These kids do not need one children's pastor; they need a hundred. Please minister arm-in-arm with me."

Be consistent. Kids are all about fair. First through third graders are especially black and white about everything. Your classroom policies will rise and fall on your team's ability to stay consistent. Whatever you say or post, you must follow through on. If you say, "Do not push others or you'll have to sit in the hallway with Frank," but you ignore the behavior and do not follow through, then you just told the entire group, "The rules we told you and the consequences we posted are really meaningless. You are not safe from others pushing you. You can push others without repercussions. We do not mean what we say." This will pull down the efficacy of your entire presentation. They will not believe what you say about Jesus is true either. As hard as it may be, you must follow through with consistency each and every time, no matter if you are tired or how busy that Sunday is. I got great advice from my college mentor that I will pass on to you.

"You need to start off being very tough, reiterating and emphasizing and focusing on the rules for your first two months at a new children's pastorate, or after implementing a new policy. Kids will test you, test the policy, and test the limits. Stay firm and loving. After those first two months, you can start to move forward, taking that group on to new levels. Whenever you have new members to the group, or you come back after a break (Christmas break, summer break), you need to go back and review the rules again and put more focus on them for a week or two to get back on track."

These are great thoughts that I continue to use to this day.

Balance: individual vs. group. You've heard me say by now how important balance is to any ministry, any minister, and to any life. Balance is so important when you're planning and implementing your ministry discipline policy. Yes, we do "leave the 99 to search for the one," but we also do not let that one harm, chase off, or eat the 99 either. Part of being a children's/family leader is having the wisdom to know when it is time to stop and show more care and ministry to that one child, and when it is time to act to protect the group as a whole. For example, a child who is grieving a loss, or going through a family separation, or abuse or neglect may need extra time, more encouragement, and a deviation from that morning's plans (as well as at-home follow-up, help, meals). However, if a child is biting, hitting, cursing, running off, creating disruptions, stealing, and interventions have already been attempted multiple times, you may have to make the tough decision to act for the safety and well-being of the group. If you don't, everyone will miss out on the most important message they could ever hear. You cannot let one ruin it for everyone. This is so hard, I know.

I suggest you put those steps in writing. Start with a warning, then move them to the back with a teacher. Talk with the parents afterwards. After a few weeks of this, sit down with the parents and a staff witness to explain in love how these issues are affecting the whole group. Let them know that one parent will have to sit one-on-one with their child for the next six weeks. After that, you will re-evaluate. Usually, they will not go for this, and will just take the child with them to the other service, so you must talk to your senior about this first. I do not make a practice of keeping a teacher of ours one-on-one with a child long-term, because we simply do not have enough leaders to spare. The parent will likely be angry and demand, "Well, you have to take him. This is church!" And your answer should be along the lines of, "We certainly love Aiden and would love to see him come back. But this is a safety issue and a major disruption problem. We must find solutions before putting him back in a classroom; this is just not working. No one knows Aiden better than you. What do you suggest we do to help him in this situation?" Listen, but continue to firmly explain that the behavior guidelines are non-negotiable, and you cannot bend them for one person without doing the same for all. Explain that you do not have enough volunteers to keep up one-on-one. Keep pointing back to the goal, which is Aiden enjoying and participating in the service without disrupting or harming someone else. Ask the parents how you can work together to make that happen. Sometimes this works and you will see an amazing turnaround for that child and even that family. Other times, the child refuses to cooperate, the parents refuse to cooperate, and eventually you will lose that child to your kids' ministry (though perhaps not permanently).

In the end, you must keep your focus on ministering the message of Jesus Christ to the kids and families God gave you to serve. You have to keep them safe while they are there. Believe me, there are a lot of other "one lost sheep" out there, and they still need you, too. Wisdom, discernment, love—for the one and for the many.

Grace. If you have to make a mistake sometime, make a mistake on the side of grace. These kids and families are going through so much … so much more than you or I ever did growing up. And if they snap at you on a Sunday morning, blow things out of proportion, mess up for the 998th time, keep offering grace. Grace does not mean condoning or allowing bad behavior. It means loving someone in spite of their behavior. And that also means saying "no" when appropriate. They are kids after all. They'll make mistakes, and don't we all? Again, be consistent with follow-through, but offer a lot of grace and love. Have you ever "won" without really "winning"? I have. Don't win one battle just to lose a war. You may get that child to finally be silent, but crush their spirit in the process; that's not a win. They may sit down now, but sit out of church later. I believe there can be a win/win—a place where the child learns rules, structure, and meaning right alongside learning all about grace. Isn't that what our walk with God is all about?

Communicating with parents. By all means possible and by all means conceivable, work as a team with the parents in ministering to their child. As a parent myself, I hate being blindsided by a teacher, such as, "Mrs. Peach, this is the 8th time in a row at school that your child has forgotten their live caught bug assignment, and if it is not turned in tomorrow at 8 am, he is getting detention!" My first thought is always, "Why is this the first I'm hearing of this? We would have made him finish it and turn it in ages ago." But I also know that children are not good at relaying messages back to parents. Parents are constantly barraged with papers from school, sports, and church. Many of those leaflets you send home get lost in the deluge of communication "white noise." How can you include more parents in the process of keeping classroom discipline?

- All children must be registered at our check-in desk. At that time, new visitors must sign a copy of our rules and policies, and we send another copy home with them. We keep their signed copy on file to refer back to should the need arise. This reading and signing of the policy statement happens also for online registrations.

- We work hard to over-communicate in every way possible, through handouts, email blasts, letters mailed to their homes, bulletins, our website, our Facebook page, announcements, videos, skywriting … well, maybe someday. Parents, grandparents, and guardians need to hear information eight or more times before it sticks, so keep letting them know!

- Post your rules and condensed policy page in many places, but especially where you know parents will see it. We have ours by the bathrooms and in the hallway where everyone checks out.

- Give parents a heads-up earlier on. I don't mean calling a parent for every hangnail. What I mean is, if it gets to the point of having to move a child to the back, or they do something dangerous, hurtful, or disrespectful, when that parent comes down for pick-up, pull them off to one side. Quietly and lovingly let them know what the issue was and how it was handled step-by-step. It doesn't take that long, and that's what you are there for anyway! To minister! Refer to the posted guidelines on the wall behind you. Ask the parent what they think would be a good next step to take. Listen to them; do not blame the parent. They may fill you in on some tough things that the child and family are facing at the present time. Smile and tell them you cannot wait to have them back next week. Pray with them right there if appropriate. Whatever you do, do not make your first approach to a parent only when you are fed up, and it's feeling like far past too late. Do not start the conversation with "And we're done." Do not assume the parent knows all about the situation you are encountering. They know their child better than you do, and they may have some great ideas for getting him/her to hear you and engage. Don't assume that non-Christian, non-churched parents do not care and will not work with you. I have found that many non-Christian parents will talk with me, and work with us if we reach out with love and respect, not in blame but in problem-solving mode. If you keep filling them in all along the way, without embarrassing or blaming them, you will make a powerful ally now and for the years to come.

Don't make church a punishment. How many times have we said or heard, "If you misbehave one more time, you're going to big church!" I cringe when I hear this, because we're making the other church service a punishment, a penalty for bad behavior, something to endure. These children begin to equate worshipping with their parents in a Sunday service as abnormal and the result of being rejected. It is a well-known fact that too many Christian children are leaving the church before they reach college age. Shouldn't we be more conscious of creating excitement about worshipping alongside other Christians? Rather than a punishment, they should see themselves as a vital part of the church—one church that expresses themselves in many ways—student ministries, outreach, community serving and more. These kids are part of the church now, and what is happening in the adult/family services should be exciting and relevant for them too. Have alternative ideas ready (sit in the hallway, sit in the back with a teacher, page their parent), but let's stop making our church's other worship services a punishment.

Don't make your senior the enemy. This goes hand-in-hand with not making the adult service a punishment. There is a problem if the only time the child sees the "boss pastor" is when they're in trouble. The lead pastor should be their pastor also, and not just used as a disciplinarian. I do not tell a child, "If you misbehave, you'll end up in the pastor's office!" In fact, we have the lead pastor in a couple of times a year to observe the kids' programs, to speak to the kids, and to have some fun with them, because he's their pastor, too. Let's not make the lead pastor someone who only interacts with that child to come down on their failures. How do the kids in your ministry feel about your lead pastor?

There are a few ideas for putting together your classroom discipline policy. This may not have been a top priority on your list, but it needs to happen so that all the kids in your ministry can have fun, make great friends … and hear and meet with Jesus. I want to show families that living by God's rules is the best way to really live! Let's do the hard work that it's going to take to create the safe place where that will happen!

CHAPTER 8
PLAYDATES WITH GOD-
DYNAMIC WORSHIP AND
ALTAR ENCOUNTERS

SATURDAY	SUNDAY
2	3 *Play date with the Almighty*
9 *Grandma's*	10 *Play date with almighty*

Little second grader Ryan sat in front of a screen in silence, watching lessons on brain surgery for one hour, every other week. The rest of the week Ryan worked on fixing things, working with his hands. When he hit high school, Ryan found a great mentor who helped him learn how to fix cars. His friends were there with him day after day learning all about cars and then they began actually fixing cars themselves. On the day he turned 18, Ryan's parents excitedly shoved a scalpel in his hand and told him to get to work as a surgeon! To their surprise, Ryan put down the scalpel and walked away with no interest at all in being a surgeon. Instead, Ryan did what he had been preparing all of his life to do, what he had spent much more of his time studying for, what he is already doing: Ryan continued to fix cars.

As ludicrous as this scenario may sound to us, all too often this is how we operate in the church today. We sit a child in front of a screen to hear about God for one hour every other week. The rest of that child's time is spent with their friends, doing something else. Why are we so surprised that so many of our churched kids turn 18, put down their faith, and walk away to continue doing what they are already doing? Are we so shocked that they cannot search the Bible for themselves? When they have no desire at all to worship, serve in the church or meet with God at all? They have no desire to meet with God, because they do not know God. You can know all about a celebrity and not know that celebrity personally. Knowing about God does not equal knowing Him.

Jesus warns that on judgment day, there will be people who did great deeds for Him, even in ministry, but He will say, *"Depart from me, for I never knew you"* (Matthew 7:23). That's such a scary scripture passage to me. There's a crucial difference there; can you see it? It's the difference between learning all the stories of the Bible and meeting the Author and knowing how to study it for yourself. It's the difference between head knowledge and heart knowledge. It's learning all the mechanics of why we worship God versus actually entering into worship of God from your heart. It's connecting who God was and what God did, with who God is and what God will do. Faith that never leaves the theoretical cannot change your heart or save your soul. Here is the simple truth we must start acting on:

> **When children move into adulthood they will in large part
> continue to do what they are already doing.**

Have you heard the saying of Aristotle, "We are what we repeatedly do"? Let's think about the kids and families we are ministering to week to week. What are they continually doing? That's who there are and who they will be in the future. The only way to change the future for these kids is to change what they're doing in their everyday lives. What this means is that their faith must be tangible. It has to have action to it. James tells us, *"Faith without works is dead"* (James 2:14). Is our faith dead? Or alive and active? Are we telling stories of what God did long ago to people far away, or are we introducing these kids to a big God who hears and sees them right now … a God who cares about them so much … a God who is active in seeking them out, forgiving, and redeeming them? Do our kids know a God who hears their prayers and answers in power? Are they aware every day that their God is actively shaping their life and their story? Do they make their decisions based on how God will feel about their actions and thoughts right now? How is their faith changing their lives every day?

Unfortunately, there are a lot of tragic misconceptions that we cling to in our churches that are blocking our younger generation from connecting with God. Have you heard or encountered any of these ministry myths for kids' and family ministry?

MYTH 1: EMOTION AND EXPERIENCE ARE NEGATIVE THINGS FOR CHILDREN AND WE NEED TO AVOID THEM IN MINISTRY.

We should focus on learning and not emotion. Since children are immature emotionally, any attempt to engage children in worship, altar time, or repentance is emotional manipulation. Churches must stick to rote learning until a child is more emotionally mature and can decide for themselves.

Truth: We Christians are always such a reactionary people—a people of extremes. Much of the thinking in the above myth is a reaction against the emotionalism in church ministry of previous decades. During that time, people in some Christian movements highlighted and valued emotion and spiritual freedom over all else. Any kind of structure, including denominations, institutionalized education and degrees, and the hierarchy of church leadership was frowned upon and distrusted. Critical thinking, planning, preparation, and routine were considered "not being led by the Spirit." Of course, this did lead to chaos at times or abuses of authority. The direct reaction to this was a total shift to the opposite extreme—no involvement of the emotions at all. For many churches this means planning services down to the millisecond, no spontaneity, no altar times, and very generic "correct" worship.

The problem with both extremes is that we are complex human beings, with a body, mind, and soul. In fact, the greatest commandment of all is: *"Love the Lord your God with all your heart, with all your mind, and with all your soul, and with all your strength"* (Luke 10:27). That means our surrender to Jesus Christ must be body, mind, soul, and emotions. Head knowledge alone is not enough. Instead of being reactionary and swinging to extremes, balance should be our key. Children are heart wired to learn through emotion and experience. God created them that way. They are seeking experiences that make the occult so much more dangerous. And kids today are, more than ever, kinesthetic learners (learning through doing). The danger here is that if you neglect ministry to the whole child, you may not get the chance to speak into their lives about Jesus ever again. Most of the time, if you wait until high school to try to engage that child for the first time in worship and prayer, you are already far too late. Everything in that child's world already pulls at their emotions. Don't make the church an exception. Yes, you can engage their emotions without manipulating or pushing. Yes, teach them to worship and then lead them into worship. Teach them all about the Bible, and then lead them to study it for themselves. Tell them about God, and then invite them to talk to Him for themselves. You must engage that child as a whole, because faith that never touches their heart is no faith at all.

MYTH 2: CHILDREN CANNOT UNDERSTAND THE DEEPER THINGS OF GOD.

Deep things of God should all wait until high school. While they are in kids' church, stick to the fun and the fluff. Keep it happy and light, because they won't face deep tragedy until much later.

Truth: Whoever said we adults understand everything about the greatness of God? We don't! We can never understand all of who He is and what He does—not even a teeny tiny portion! Yet, we are invited to get to know Him personally. Don't shy away from the heavy things of God with these young ones! They can handle it, sometimes better than the adults. Don't downplay their great faith. I've seen among Christians the erroneous thinking that, "Spiritual things should be kept from children until they are older and better able to understand them." This kind of thinking is exactly opposite from what God has laid out in Scripture. We're to start as young as possible introducing them to Jesus Christ.

Why is it so crucial that we do not shy away from the heavy stuff? Many of these children have experienced more tragedy, more loss, more bullying in their very young lives than you or I have in our lives combined. If statistics fall true in your church, then almost half of the children you minister to are from divorced families, blended families, or single-parent homes. In some areas that number is much higher. Many of the kids you minister to have been abused or neglected. That is just a fact. These kids have many times experienced a death of someone close to them or bullying in their schools. And to me, children seem so much more hopeless than they did when I was younger. An 11-year-old boy in my son's school system committed suicide last month. I have trouble wrapping my mind around a child that young giving up hope on life. But this world is a much different place than the one you and I grew up in. These kids need to know they can go to God—not later on in life, but right now. Children in your ministry need to be equipped to handle the heavy stuff life throws at them, with knowledge and experience of a God who loves them and cares. If you will not address the tougher subjects with kids, they will find their answers elsewhere, and that should scare us. If all we show kids is fun and fluff, they will see Christianity as one more fictional fun drama for them to watch, not at all pertaining to their real life. Be honest or they will not trust you! They already know life includes suffering and loss; show them that God is God over all of our lives—the fun stuff and the tough stuff.

MYTH 3: I SHOULD NOT TALK TO THE KIDS ABOUT MY PERSONAL JOURNEY OR EXPERIENCES WITH GOD. THEY WOULD NOT BE ABLE TO UNDERSTAND.

Look at Deuteronomy 6:6-7: *"Keep these words that I am commanding you today in your heart. Recite them to your children and talk about them when you are at home and when you are away, when you lie down and when you rise."* There are many such commands in God's Word to tell children all about the wonderful things God has done and said. The command was not limited to parents! It was the parents' first responsibility yes, to tell their children about the love and law of God, but it was the whole congregation's duty to keep retelling the stories of God's goodness to all of the children! The Israelites disobeyed God's command to instruct their children, and the result was: *"Another generation grew up after them, who did not know the Lord or the work that he had done for Israel. Then the Israelites did what was evil in the sight of the lord ... they abandoned the Lord"* (Judges 2:10-11a). These children grew up never knowing God, or how He delivered their grandparents from slavery, or how He parted the Red Sea for their parents to walk through on dry ground. They never learned anything about the Lord, so when they grew up, they chose to have nothing to do with God. How sad!

As we look back on our lives, and a church history so full of healing, growth, and miracles, I wonder, do our children know all of the wonderful things GOD has done for us? Do they know how we first met Jesus?

Answer me this. Do the children in your ministry know your personal story of meeting and walking with Jesus? How about the stories of your key leaders? I'm not talking about all the gritty details that would be inappropriate for them right now. But it is crucial that they know the life change in you and their leaders, not just people in the past.

When God answers a prayer for us, be it financial, physical, or spiritual, do we let our children know God cares enough about us to answer with power? I believe that when our children reach the age of accountability, they will each make their decision concerning Jesus Christ based on their experiences up to that point. We cannot make that decision for them. But we can shape their early experiences to point them to Jesus. When John the Baptist sent his disciples to Jesus to ask, *"Are You the Christ or do we look for another?"* Jesus did not give them all a lesson in systematic theology, or assign them a great book to read. He simply said, *"Go tell John what you hear and see: the blind receive their sight, the lame walk, the lepers are cleansed, the deaf hear, the dead are raised, and the poor have the good news preached to them"* (Matthew 11:4).

When our children ask us, "Is Jesus the answer, or do we look for another?" (and if they don't ask out loud, they will think it some time in their lives), we need to be prepared to tell them over and over the wonderful things God has done for us—both in the past and this week. If we honestly cannot think of anything recent to tell—no current answers to prayer—then we must pray for more, believe God to reveal Himself in the here and now. When God answers in a big way, remember that your testimony of God's goodness in front of the church on the weekend will never be as important as your testimony in your mini-van on the way to or from church. Go be that living message to these kids! We have a command and a duty to tell the kids in our ministry what God has done for and in us!

MYTH 4: WORSHIP AND ALTAR TIMES ARE JUST FOR CAMP.
Truth: Encounters with God should become part of our everyday lives.

I love Bible camp, but you don't eat once a year, and you shouldn't feed your soul once a year. You can have amazing worship and altar times right at your church if you are willing to work hard, rehearse, and craft that service. Your church kids should not have to go off to camp to have an experience with God. That kind of thinking fosters a life that compartmentalizes God into certain activities and certain times of year only. God should be in charge year round everywhere we go! They should be ready to worship, pray, and be changed in God's presence every time your group gets together!

This does take time, training, and patience however. If your kids' church learned to do things one way, they can be retrained to worship and pray. It took us the better part of a year to teach and train our kids to be an active part of our worship and altar time. Internationally known kids' pastor, John Tasch, always says that children should be taught how to worship, how to pray, and how to serve, just like we would teach them to make a bed. We teach children to ride a bike. We don't just expect them to learn balance through osmosis. If you work with kids to show them how and why we worship and pray, they are very quick learners. Don't give up. Keep trying to lead them deeper.

MYTH 5: ONLY ADULTS CAN BE LEADERS IN WORSHIP OR HELP PRAY WITH PEOPLE.
Truth: The goal is to lead your group of kids from passive recipients to active participants.

If you watch the same shows these kids are watching every day on Nickelodeon, Disney XD, etc. those actors are not adults. They are teenagers and older kids. As we explained in book one, the kids you minister to do not want to be you. They desperately want to be teenagers. Whatever the teenagers do this week, your group of kids will be doing next week. Do whatever you can to incorporate teenagers, college age, and grade schoolers in your worship team and altar team. Kids will follow what they see teenagers doing anyway, so give them role models you want them to follow. And yes, I pair our teens and kids with outstanding adult leaders who model passionate, effective worship, and serving. Before long, the kids on our team begin doing the ministry for themselves—singing worship to God from their hearts, crying and praying with a friend whose mother is sick, or sharing a verse of scripture or a testimony. The amazing thing is that as these kids and youth minister, all of the other kids are listening and 100% engage and follow their lead. Sometimes the best person to minister to a child is someone who is or just was in their shoes.

The limits of a child's ministry are really just the ones we decide to impose. Instead of thinking that adults are ministering to the kids, we need a paradigm shift, where our kids' church becomes a ministry center/training ground for all of us to discover our gifts and learn to minister in love to each other. This will cause your ministry to grow in effectiveness and numbers. How can you include more children and youth in your kids' ministry?

MYTH 6: DECISIONS THAT A CHILD MAKES DURING AN ALTAR SERVICE OR WORSHIP TIME WILL NOT STICK. IT'S ALL JUST EMOTION.

Truth: As you may know, 80% of people who are actively serving Jesus today made that decision as a child under the age of 12. And it stuck.

I was 4 years old when I decided to follow Christ. I knew exactly what I was praying for that day. I knew I was a sinner, that Jesus died for me, and that I needed His forgiveness in order to live my life for Him. We should not discount a child's decisions. I had an 8-year-old girl tell me she was going to be a missionary. A couple people laughed. I did not. That young lady is now a missionary overseas. It is not our job to judge which decisions are "real" or "all emotion." We just set up the meeting between them and God. It's not your job to save anyone; that's the Holy Spirit's job. But I am very careful not to discount a child's decision to accept Christ, or to serve, or to change something in their lives.

MYTH 7: KIDS' WORSHIP IS FUN, SILLY, AND CUTE ... AND THE KIDS DON'T CARE IF IT'S POLISHED.

Truth: We don't give God our garbage.

From miles away, kids can spot a fake or something sloppy that's thrown together. They live in a world with the very best in graphics, stories, and talent. You don't have to be perfect, but they will know if you cared enough to prepare. Yes, kids' worship can be funny and crazy, but then it needs to go deeper to a heart level. To skip the deeper aspects of worship is to waste one of the most important parts of your entire kids' service. This is what separates a fun connecting time from a dynamic kids' church service—worship and altar time. A high level of quality and preparation tells your audience that this message matters—to you, your team, and to them. We have the most important message anywhere of all time. My rule has always been, "If it's not our best, we won't do it. If you don't practice, you don't go on." And kids rise to that challenge!

So if you're convinced that we need now, more than ever, to work towards dynamic worship and altar times in our local churches on a weekly basis, how do you start making that happen?

Proven Strategies for Making Your Kids' Worship and Altar Time More Effective
Be specific, not abstract in what you're asking the children in your group to do. Kids do not do well with anything vague or abstract (and most adults don't either). Here are a few examples of vague sermon, altar, and worship appeals I've heard recently. Have you heard these?

- Go ahead and come up to the altar if you feel led. (Would a child understand that?)

- As we stand just make the decision you need to make. (What decision? Do I need to make it?)

- Go be more loving. (Huh? Where are we going? How do we do that? To whom? By when?) These answers are not always obvious to everyone.

- All of you guys go worship God in your own way. (This method is not usually a good one for kids. They need a bit more direction. Trust me.)

- If there's anything in your life right now that needs prayer, we're here. (How does the child know what to do here? Go up there to you? How do they know if they should ask for prayer? What things can they ask prayer for?)

More specific asks I've heard.
- Can we pray with you for the courage to share Jesus this week? Think of one friend that you know needs to know Jesus. We want to pray with you, for God-given courage to share Christ with them. In two minutes, I'm going to ask you to go find your leader and take a minute to share the name of that friend, and they will pray with you.

- I want each one of you to show the love of Jesus to someone before Wednesday. I'll ask you guys on Wednesday how it went. We will end today making a card for you to give to someone who is sick, in the hospital, or in a nursing home.

- Sometimes we struggle with one thing that seems to have us in a strangle hold—lying, cheating, anger, disrespecting parents, bullying, hating. Are you ready to win this battle? Can I pray with you for God's help in defeating your own personal battle? You don't need to tell us what it is, but you should tell your parents. They can help you win that battle, too! If you've thought of one wrong action that you need to get rid of from your life, come up here to your leader and let's pray together.

- We've learned that we must forgive just like Jesus forgave and continues to forgive. Who are you having a hard time forgiving today? Can I pray with you so that you have the power to forgive the one who hurt you?

Remember, repetition is okay and is, in fact, necessary to make something a habit. Children need repetition. So it's okay and even advisable to reuse the same worship songs over and over. I don't recommend doing all new songs every week. It just leads to frustration and kids checking out. We add, at most, only 1 or 2 new songs per month. Let them get comfortable with the songs so they can concentrate on worship and prayer. You'll need to repeat your rules for behavior during worship and prayer time. You'll also need to repeat your prayer and message topics on subjects that these kids really need to hear: salvation, bullying, forgiveness, family, worship, Bible study. We intentionally speak on salvation at least ten times every year, if not more.

Remove the barriers between God and His kids. He wants to be with them more than you want them with Him. Remove distractions, especially at first. You can let up a bit later. I don't allow any walking around, leaving, random talking, or horseplay during worship or altar time. I'm very serious that this is the most important time and the real reason we are all here—to meet with and hear from God and to minister to each other. Work to get rid of noises, flashing lights, smells—anything that would distract. I also don't allow costumed characters or puppets during this time because they command too much attention. I don't have anyone playing, or any toys out, or any prizes on the stage. Keep the focus on God during worship and altar time. Discourage parents from marching up front and taking their child out. It's extremely distracting (and disrespectful, but some families do not know any better yet.) I have signs posted at the back of our room that say, "Shhhh! We're finishing up our time with God. We will be with you in just a moment." It took a bit of time to train our church people, but now, parents do wait patiently in the back of the room in the pick-up line until we're done. The huge wins for us have been:

- It has added perceived value to our ministry in the eyes of the parents and our leaders, because they see children not in childcare, but in a kids' church service.

- Parents get to see exactly what their children are learning/doing and can reinforce it at home!

- The kids stay on task until we're done with the service. We don't abuse this and try to end plus or minus 5 minutes from the end of the adult service.

Do not bar or shame a child from coming up repeatedly. I saw a little girl go up to the front a few weeks ago to pray for her grandma's arm. The well-meaning pastor said to her, "Oh honey, we already prayed for that last week." The girl turned beet red and retreated to her seat. I wonder how long it will take that girl to work up the courage to ask for prayer from someone again, if ever. Jesus said, *"Let the children come to Me and forbid them not."* Children were not a hassle or a distraction in Jesus' ministry. I'll point out that that Scripture also says, *"Ask, seek, and knock."* Perhaps, we adults would see more answers to prayer if we didn't give up so easily! If a child comes up every single week to pray for their mom's smoking problem? Then, you sincerely pray with that child every week for their mother. Do not do anything to damage that child's faith. Do not make that child feel that God is irritated with their asking … or that they are being barred access to Him … or that they are an annoyance to God or to you. We should be so thankful that when they have a problem, they're going to God, and to their church leaders, and to their parents for prayer! How would our churches be different if our adults did that?

One of my leaders prayed with a young boy whose dog had run away in a city over an hour away on their family's camping trip. She said, "I felt kinda silly praying for a dog that had been missing for almost a month. I mean, I knew the chances of Ben coming home were next to none. But Ian was so upset I just prayed with him anyway." Two weeks later, Ian gave a testimony in kids' church, "I asked Jesus to do a miracle and bring Ben home. I went to church and they prayed with me about Ben. Last week, someone called us from an hour away; they found Ben and brought him home. We still don't know how they found us! Now

I know for sure that there is a God and He is listening." I cried. This meant the whole world to this little boy and his eternal soul. (I have prayed for so many hamsters, goldfish, and lizards too by the way.) Do not ever downplay a child's prayer request, no matter how small it seems to you, or how many times they are coming to God with it. Know that God will use that situation, just because they are coming to Him!

Don't manipulate. You should never need to force kids to enter into worship or altar time. You can lead them in that direction, but let them go at their own pace. I do not force kids to come up, or pray out loud, or sing out loud if they don't want to. Some children are more shy or introverted, and I don't want them to have a terrible experience with worship, prayer, or any part of church. God loves all of His kids, even the less demonstrative ones! The biggest way that manipulation sneaks into our kids' services is in our altar appeals. Have you heard these?

- "Well, if you love Jesus, then just get up here to this altar." (So if you stay seated, are you are publicly declaring that you don't?)

- "If you have sinned, stand up." (Good grief. All have sinned! That's kinda cheap!)

- "I will keep waiting here until you all have the courage to get up here!" (That's still pretty vague, especially when you're dealing with kids. I don't believe an appeal like this explains why they should come for prayer or why they should change.)

Usually, when a kids' ministry speaker gives a worship or prayer appeal that is full of vague requests or guilt, shaming, goading, or threats, it's not that the speaker is intentionally trying to manipulate kids. More often than not the speaker is just inexperienced, nervous, or unsure how to end the service. Sometimes, the speaker has been taught to feel like a failure unless "everyone comes to the front." Notice that Jesus said, "Let the children come to Me", not "Drag the children," or "Shove the children," or "Threaten and shame the children all the way to Me." When we simply remove all the barriers and distractions, model passionate worship and prayer, and teach children how to connect with God, they are naturally drawn by the Spirit of God! In our ministry, I see kids "get it" and enter into worship and prayer much faster than adults, probably because they do not have as many defenses and scarring built up against God as some adults do. Open the door for the kids in your ministry to enter in and meet with God. Make the way as amazing and easy to access as possible. You won't need to shove them in. They'll go running.

Make it the norm to meet with God and go to Him when we have need. Make it feel weird not to go to God. Just like our kids have been trained (in some churches) to sit, listen, or watch a video, they can be trained to worship, pray, and study their Bibles. It's been said that anything you do for six weeks or more becomes a habit. We can create an environment where listening to God, living for God, and meeting with God are the realities of everyday life. You start by modeling this. When there is a tragedy, a disaster, or a loss, let them see you pray and take it to God. Are there big decisions to make? As a group, take it to God. Find answers in Scripture together.

When the kids come into kids' church right now, what are they expecting? Fun games? Lights? Hilarious characters? That's great. They can also come in expecting an amazing time of worship, a chance to be prayed for, and to pray for others. It's all about what you decide to make the standard for your kids' ministry. I want every child in our ministry to grow up in such a way that when they go to college they will have to find a place to worship and serve as soon as possible, because it will feel so weird and abnormal to live life apart from the family of God.

I think we all can be passionate about seeing heart change in the kids we minister to. So no matter how your curriculum is set up, mercilessly cut whatever else you have to in order to make time for worship and prayer. Never ever cut those. They should be why you're there. Snacks, games, and rote memorization are fun, but they won't change anyone's heart for eternity. Time spent in God's presence will. We have the greatest job in the whole wide world—setting up reunions between God and His kids. God is more than

ready and willing. He's waiting. It's our job to craft a service that makes everything—and everyone—come together in knowledge, sometimes emotionally, and be forever changed in His presence.

CHAPTER 9
THE DISCIPLED CHILD—GRADUATION DAY

Pastor Joshua squirmed in his seat on the stage. There were so many kids moving up to their new classes on this church-wide graduation day that this service was taking forever. One at a time, each child crossed the stage to a lot of cheering and applause to receive their Year Completion Certificate. They stopped at center stage to shake hands with their teacher so their parents could get pictures. This was always a big day especially for the 5th graders who would now be graduating up into student ministries. Some of these 5th graders were excited and so eager to move up; they couldn't wait to be at youth group this coming Wednesday night. Other children were more nervous about leaving kids' church for student ministries, worried about all the new teachers, new formats, and new environment. Both groups of 5th graders seemed a little bit sad to see a chapter in their lives coming to a close … a really great chapter … one that had changed their lives in ways they will never forget!

With a start, Pastor Joshua was jolted out of his revere by the volunteer leader sitting to his left. Tom was a 13-year veteran of the children's ministry at Zion kids and was one of the most faithful, dedicated servants they had on their team. "Pastor Josh," Tom whispered. "Isn't this just something? It always chokes me up to see these kids graduate up, you know?"

"Oh yeah. Sure. We'll definitely miss them." Joshua whispered back just to make conversation.

"Have you ever thought about it Pastor Josh? We have so little time, really, with each one of these kids. And then they are gone, out of our influence, in the blink of an eye! How do we know we did it right? How do we know they got everything they needed to make it as a Christian in middle school … and for the rest of their lives? Are they where they need to be for this graduation?"

Pastor Joshua coughed and then blinked three times. What a question to ask! But before Joshua shot back a pat answer, he began to think to himself. As he watched Jules Dawson walk across the stage, smile to her parents and accept her certificate, that picture of 11-year-old Jules froze in his mind. How do we know we properly equipped these kids? As she now walks off the stage and into middle school, have we prepared her to defend her faith, search Scripture for herself, pray, and worship as her own person? Does she know she is a vital part of our church? And the deeper question rose to the surface of his mind, "For all of the children in our programs right now, are we preparing them for a lifetime relationship with Jesus Christ? How will we know? What would that look like? Can we describe a child who is entering their teenage years with a healthy biblical worldview and a solid Christian walk?" Pastor Joshua did not answer Tom right away. This was a huge question—a question he would need to start exploring, starting now.

How about you? Can you relate to Pastor Joshua's dilemma? Have you ever wondered if you are fully preparing each child in their faith? We all should be. Gone are the days of children making those big spiritual decisions mainly in youth group. Children are finalizing their views of right and wrong younger and younger. According to George Barna in *Transforming Children into Spiritual Champions*, a child has already shaped most of their views of right and wrong, the nature of God, and their moral view of the world by the age of nine! As we already talked about in book one, we only have these kids an average of 1 hour per week, only 32 days a year. That's only 32 hours to try to make a huge impact for life. These statistics should scare us and challenge us. We must be incredibly intentional about our programming to do everything we can to equip these kids in every way possible. Part of that equipping process must include partnering with the parents to make sure that these kids are getting what they need spiritually at home first, where they spend the most time. Parents + church + dedicated Christian friends make a dynamic support structure for optimal change and growth.

Another part of this process is learning to do a more successful handoff of kids from children's ministry to student ministries. By and large, there is a problem in most churches when it comes time for kids to graduate into youth group. The statistics are pretty scary. Why the huge drop-off? Too many times churches will start the blame game here: "The youth group is too boring," "The youth group kids are too wild and are a bad influence," "The music is too loud," "The kids just miss kids' church too much," "The kids' church was too unstructured and undisciplined and the kids can't handle structure now," "The kids' team is negative about youth group and discourages the kids." As we already pointed out, blame doesn't get it done. You and your team need to step out and change the paradigm from blame storming to brain storming. Only the children and families suffer when teams are divided and blaming each other. How can the families, the pastors, the leaders, and the volunteers work together to make the transition smoother and keep your kids in church? Here are a few ideas we've been using.

Bring the youth pastor(s) in several times to speak, be interviewed, and meet with the kids throughout the year. I even have our two youth pastors at our outreach events and special fun nights. Encourage them to get to know the kids and let the kids get to know the youth pastors long before moving up.

Don't let it become a competition. In every way, strive to work as ministry teams, working for the same goals. Don't get territorial. If a teenager wants to serve in student ministries A/V instead of nursery, just be glad they are still enjoying serving in their church! And if a teenager wants to help in pre-k, praise God they are serving in church! I have student leaders who serve in every area of children's ministry, and they are amazing. Most churches make students wait until they are at least three years older than the kids in that class to be a helper. I have all student ministers sign a conduct contract explaining exactly what they are committing to, and it must be signed by their parents and their student pastor. If their student pastor tells me that the student is skipping a lot of church or breaking contract by acting inappropriately, I take it seriously and act on that immediately. Those who refuse to cooperate with teamwork and accountability have to step down from ministry. No matter what, the kids and families need to see the whole family life ministry area as one solid team, not several teams all fighting over members.

Have visiting nights before the graduation weekend when 5th graders can experience a youth group service. Plan this night carefully with the youth pastor to make sure it's a dazzling, fun night.

Have conversations with your youth pastor/team about strategies to really plug these new younger kids right into youth group. What is the plan for follow-up? Can they be assigned buddies to sit with? Are there serving opportunities they can start on right away? How can you be preparing them now for that youth experience? What is the plan if a child starts missing youth group after a few weeks? If both teams are open to having these discussions, the results can be powerful.

Have events all year that combine the two groups. We do "Club 45" which includes 4th, 5th, and 6th graders in fun nights (mini-golf, pizza and gaming). We do these six times a year, with the children's and student leaders all present and working together. This helps our 4th and 5th graders make a few friends in student ministries too!

Curb the negative talk. There will be children, parents, and leaders who will come to you to complain about the student ministries. They will say they don't want to go or their child doesn't want to go. Do not be a safe place for that kind of talk. Always build up the student ministries team and back them, publicly and privately, even when you don't agree with some of their calls. Keep encouraging the kids to get into student ministries, to make friends, and find a place to serve. Urge the parents to serve in student ministries and to pray for their student pastors and leaders. It is not a win for your ministry if those kids you poured into start hanging out of church, no matter what the reason. Pour into them again by urging them to get to church and stay involved. If they complain about something (ie., it's boring, the kids are wild, I'm not fed), then help them find a way to get involved and be an agent for change, helping their student ministries' leaders, not being a part of the problem.

Celebrate and make a big deal when a child graduates up to student ministries. Let them know you're proud of them, that this is part of growing up, and that a whole new exciting chapter in their lives is beginning. Do not make it a funeral or a sad thing. Don't make it sound like the end of fun. Talk up all the great things they will now be able to be a part of!

BOTTOM LINE: It is mission critical that we work together to do our graduation handoffs well.

That brings us back to our original question. How do we know that we have fully equipped a child spiritually to go into youth group? What is the goal? What does the fully discipled child look like? What does that child sound like? The answer to these questions should guide us in every decision we make in children's ministry from curriculum, to service structure, to what we choose to emphasize week to week.

I realize that this list will not be comprehensive. But when I visualize a child, age 11-12, graduating out of children's ministries into student ministries, this is what I and my teams are looking for, fighting for, and planning for every week, Sunday after Sunday. Here are our goals in no particular order.

By the Grace of God: A Child Graduating Out of Our Kids' Ministry

... will know what they believe and why.

They will be able to accurately and positively defend their faith (apologetics). A child in grade school is the best they will ever be in their entire lives at committing things to memory. We should not waste a moment of this key time for helping children learn and memorize what matters most. In fact, a lot of people will tell you that they memorized most of the Scripture they know now, before the age of 12.

I had a talk with a Mom recently who informed me that she would not be bringing her young son to church. She said that she felt a child was too young to learn things about God and the Bible, and that when he turned 18, she would let him choose for himself if he wanted to start going to church. I looked at her and asked, "So are you keeping him out of school as well? Perhaps when he is 18 you should let him decide if he should start school or not. He is far too young to understand everything they teach in school, too. And definitely do not take him to the pediatrician. Just wait until he's 18 and let him decide if he wants to visit the doctor and start his vaccinations." She instantly snapped, "Well 18 is far too late to start school and way too late to start his vaccinations! He has to start now or he'll be way behind! He may not like school, but that's too bad. He has a lot to learn." I responded,

"Exactly, Mae. Your child's spiritual health, spiritual journey is the most important part of your child's life ... far too important to be neglected or left off to the wayside. Did you know that by the age of 12 Jack is going to make most of his life's decisions about right and wrong and what he believes? You want him to make all of his choices in a moral void? Or entirely based on DisneyXD and his 5th grade friend's opinions? You are the parent, and you have to make those decisions for him until he is ready. This is a crucial time; don't waste it, because there isn't a second chance." To my delight, she really thought about what I said, and so far has routinely been bringing her son to church.

How important is learning to defend their faith and knowing what they believe? Never have our kids had to defend their beliefs so early. Gone are the days of certain issues only popping up in high school or middle school. Children in elementary school are facing discussions about Islam and atheism by the third grade. Homosexuality is being discussed younger and younger. Children in our kids' church routinely tell me things like, "My teacher says it is illogical to believe in God." "My teacher says that I am just too influenced by my pastors and my parents. I need to think for myself and not out of an old book" (which I found so insulting). "My teacher says that all religions are the same and say the same things." "Two of my friends at school say they are atheists. What do I do?" "A good friend has asked me to explain why Jesus died on the cross, and how do I know He came back from the dead? What do I say?" These are the issues our kids are facing, so isn't it cruel to send them into those challenges day after day without the tools to respond? I suggest offering classes, retreats, dialoguing, and dramas all about sharing their faith in love, and how to respond when someone asks questions or even teases them about being a Christian. One of the most important things we can do for our kids is to teach them what we believe, why we believe it, and how to effectively articulate, defend, and share those beliefs. When they leave our program, we want every child to be able to explain what we believe, and why, and defend it using scriptures.

… will be as prepared as possible for a positive transition to student ministries.
(See my previous comments.)

… will know their major Bible stories and have a working knowledge of God's Word.
They will be able to search Scripture for themselves to find the answers they need. This is important. We want the children to go from being fed beliefs and scriptures, to digging in and finding these treasures for themselves. We want to instill a lifelong love of God's Word and a daily habit of reading and studying it.

… can spot cults and false doctrine and knows why they are false.
This goes right along with knowing what we believe and why. More and more cults are targeting children. It is more important now than ever that our kids can search the Bible for themselves and recognize a false doctrine when they come across it.

... has solid Christian friendships that hopefully will go with him into student ministries.

One common denominator that has kept kids in church longer is having a network of kids their age they identify with and surround themselves with. We want each child to make solid Christian friends and to learn to be a positive Christian friend to others. Living in a community of believers, growing together in Jesus is what church is all about! We intentionally work to foster these friendships, to provide positive peer pressure, accountability, and a "net" to keep kids from slipping through the cracks and out of our doors. We want normal life for every child as they grow up to include worshipping together with their friends.

... is actively serving in the church.

We want our kids to love their church and feel very much a part of it—right now. We should help each child their their gifts and how to use them in ministry! We should always be looking for new ways to use our talents for God and others—at church, at home, and in our community. Over and over again, I've found this to be true: The children you involve will be the children you keep. You cannot expect them to sit around until they are 25 staring at the wall and then suddenly join the deacon board. If you wait too long, they are already gone. Children who are involved in serving are much more likely to stay in church and stay committed even through rocky church times and transitions. Involve them right now! Create opportunities for the kids and their families in your ministry to reach out using their gifts. A life of serving should be the routine for every Christian; it should be normal for these kids to join student ministries and immediately look for their place to help out. The child who is graduating up should be a child excited to minister!

... has surrendered their life to Jesus.

This includes a dynamic commitment to live life God's way. This child will have a biblical view of the world, of right and wrong, and of the family. In everything, this child will be thinking, "What does God want?" When they consider their future, they are thinking, "What does God have for me to do?" God takes center stage over all else. This also translates into the child's attitude and actions reflecting the fruit of the Spirit. This is a child working to be more and more like Jesus.

... has had several experiences of God's presence.

God is a very real Person in their life on a daily basis—not an impersonal, historical, or mythical figure. Theirs is a vibrant relationship with a living God. This is just as crucial, if not more so, than making sure each child has the head knowledge of God. Heart knowledge needs to be happening week-to-week as well. The child who is graduating up knows how to pray for themselves and others. They will have had prayers answered. They cannot be convinced that God does not exist, because they have seen God in action in their lives and on their behalf. The desire will be there for more of God's presence in their lives through worship, water and Spirit baptism, scripture, serving, and more. When crisis hits, they will turn to God for help. This child believes and has an active vital relationship with a big God, who listens, cares, and acts on their behalf.

... is missions minded—a giver.

We want our kids to leave our programs with a giving nature that is directly counter-cultural to our mainly selfish, materialistic human nature. Each child will learn to tithe and to give. They will make it a habit to give to and serve the poor, the hurting, the hungry, soldiers, the imprisoned, Christians suffering around the world for their faith, and those in the hospital. When there is a natural disaster or community crisis, these kids will be thinking, "How can I show the love of Christ? How can I help?" These are kids who will give sacrificially of time, money, things, and service. Instead of hoarding stuff for themselves, they will think of their possessions as gifts God has entrusted to them to use for good.

When we sit down to plan our year of ministry, we have all of the above in our minds. All of these are considered when we pick out curriculum, plan events, and evaluate our progress. You cannot ever get "there" if you don't know where "there" is—where you are going.

Take a moment here with me. Visualize the children in your ministry right now. Imagine you're standing there watching them graduate into student ministry, which very soon you will. What are you truly hoping for in the lives of these kids? What are their parents hoping to instill in these kids before then? Most importantly, what do you believe God really, really wants them to know? Write what you think. You will want to refer back to this often. At the very least, I want you to start thinking with the end goals in mind.

_____

_____

_____

_____

_____

_____

How does this picture of the child graduating out of your program become reality? What do you need to do differently to make these goals happen? _____

_____

_____

Once again, I want to thank you from the bottom of my heart for going on this journey with me. My heart is full of joy and excitement at the amazing job we get to do—lead these precious kids to Jesus and watch them grow! What a gift it is that God chose us to get to do this most important work! Thank you for being willing to pour into the lives of beautiful, broken children and families. May God continue to bless and grow your ministry. With fresh inspiration, let's jump in all the more and never ever give up.

For Jesus and His kids,
Love, Trisha

Wait ... Whatever happened to Joshua—the first-time children's pastor we introduced in Chapter One? After a year in the ministry, he addressed his team at the volunteer appreciation banquet, and this is what he had to say.

I want to thank all of you, from the bottom of my heart, for being here tonight. I know that most of you on our team do not like to be recognized. You're always serving, so it probably feels weird to be served. But we designed this night to say thank you to you—our volunteers and partners in this ministry. If you'll give me a moment, there are some specific things I need to thank you for right now.

Thank you for sticking with our kids and family ministry during a year of a lot of transition. I know many of you loved and supported Pastor Carl, and I am so glad you have stepped in to support me and my wife, too. I want to be honest with you right now and say that this was a lot harder than I originally anticipated. There were so many twists and turns this year. I've learned so much—some of it the hard way—but I love this ministry and still wouldn't trade it for the world. We know that some people did leave during this time, and we sent them out with our blessing. I'm so thankful for those of you who stuck it out, helping us, and supporting us through this time.

Thank you to everyone who helped with our newly renovated kids' worship center! Thank you for your patience during the construction and your willingness to move classes around … and even outside during our VBS! Thank you for giving of your artistic talents and bringing these worship spaces far beyond anything I could ever have imagined. I heard families in the hallway this Sunday saying, 'Wow, that's exciting!' and "My friend's family should see this." We know that all the hard work, patience, and sacrifice paid off, because we not only met our goals for growing our area, we exceeded them! What will we do when we fill up our new worship spaces? Yikes. I'll pray about that!

Thank you to everyone who helped with our summer VBS. It was such a huge job and your first one with me at the helm. I couldn't have done it without you guys. Thank you for talking me off the ledge the week before. That was rough. But again, we exceeded our goals for reaching new families, and I just had to share with you some of the best news I have heard all year. My follow-up team let me know that of the 31 new families that

attended our VBS, 14 have begun regularly attending our church! I know! Six of the kids who accepted Christ in our worship and altar time last week were kids from those families. Great job with that, altar team; you served with such grace last Sunday. Our outreach was definitely worth all that work. I'm glad we have already started early on next year's.

Thank you to our weekend kids' ministry teams. You nailed the four weeks after the VBS. That's teamwork! I'm so excited to see the drama, costumed characters, puppetry, and worship keep improving every single week in kids' church. This next year I want to add elements, such as a kids' choir, dance team, and a kid greeter team. How can we involve even more kids in ministry? I'm hearing the best news of all from parents, that these kids who are at our altars, worshipping, and serving, are showing a true heart and total life change. They are sharing their faith! And isn't that what it's all about?

I want to thank our student pastor for attending tonight's volunteer thank you rally. You rock man! All of us are excited for the upcoming "Step Up to Student" night. These sixth graders are so excited! Thank you, Ben, for finding these new students places to serve in student ministries.

I want to thank each of you who went the extra mile when little Kylie died. We were all hit so hard by her loss—teachers, kids, and parents alike. I know that we all prayed for her to get better. I was so not ready to deal with her loss; I had no idea what to tell the kids at first. But I believe that our whole team, and our kids' church, bonded together even stronger during that time. Thank you for being willing to go to the grief trainings with me. It helped me grow a lot as a leader. We have been through a lot together this year, but we're a stronger team knowing that God has brought us this far.

And finally, thank you for signing on for this next year of kids' and family ministry here at Hope Church. I really do not know what all lies ahead for this next year. I'm sure we'll face challenges; and I'm sure we'll be strong through those challenges. Thank you for partnering with me to reach kids and families in our area. What an amazing adventure! And though I do not know everything about where this year will take us, I can hardly wait to get started."

Family/Participant Agreement
"Hero High" Musical

Thank you so much for being a part of our next kids' and family outreach. As with "Joy Story," "High School Miracle," and "sCARS," we're trying some very ambitious things as far as choreography and technical production. There are only a certain number of scheduled rehearsals and it is very important for every member of the team to be at the rehearsals. Please understand that it may become (in fact, it is more than likely) necessary to add extra rehearsals closer to the actual event. Enclosed is a form for absences that you know will be happening. Please let us know as soon as you can, so we can plan accordingly.

Note: Junior/Senior High Retreats will not count as a skip.
Attendance will be taken at every rehearsal. We have understudies for most speaking roles. Each member is allowed a maximum of six skipped practices. On the seventh skip, that member will be removed from the production and the understudy will take over. All parts and roles are important; every solo, alter worker, AV and tech person are all needed. We want to give God our very best in every way. More important than our talents, abilities, and flash onstage is our attitude and conduct. If a team member constantly shows a bad attitude, language and/or, un-Christ-like behavior either at church or at home, ON OR OFF THE STAGE, it may be grounds for dismissal from the production.

Most importantly, be praying that God will really use this team to reach whole families for Jesus. Thank you all so much. We look forward to partnering with you all this year. God is going to do great things for families who need Jesus in the Dayton area.
God Bless,

Pastor Trisha, Children's Pastor
Laura Tubman, Ministry Assistant

_____   _____
     (Team Member Signature)   (Parent/Guardian Signature)

_____   _____
         (date)   (Student Ministries Signature)

SAMPLE: SUMMER REHEARSAL/OUTREACH SCHEDULE

PowerHouse Church

Parent/Participant Summer Outreach Schedule

Lead roles/drama/dance rehearsals: Noon-2 pm, West Auditorium, Connection Center

Choir: with Robin Spencer and Aaron Svisco

May 5	All speaking characters' costume fitting #1, SLC 4 pm. Scripts handed out!
May 12	Costume fitting #2, first video promo shoot rehearsal, all speaking characters, SLC 3 pm
May 19	Costume fitting, full make-up and hair, final video shoot, headshot photo shoot for promotional materials, all speaking characters, 10 am
June 12-13	Rehearsal, first scene memorized. Dance number "I Need a Hero"
June 19-20	Rehearsals 12-2 pm
June 26-27	Rehearsals with all lines MEMORIZED!
July 3	Rehearsals (last work for the parade) July 4th OFF!
July 6	7 pm, Dayton Airshow Parade
July 10-11	Rehearsal
July 17-18	Rehearsal
July 24-25	Rehearsal
July 31, Aug. 1	Rehearsal
Aug. 7-8	Rehearsal, Final rehearsal EAP
AUGUST 11	Englewood Arts Parade
Aug. 14-15	Rehearsal, last weekday rehearsals! Dress rehearsal for Partner Church performance
Aug. 19	Partner performance, dress rehearsal Aug 18 in the evening
Aug. 26	Dress Rehearsal Little York, Main Sanctuary, 3-9 pm
Aug. 28	Band dress rehearsal, 6 pm, Main Sanctuary
Aug. 29	Full Dress and Tech Rehearsal, 6 pm, Main Sanctuary
Aug. 31	"HERO HIGH", Little York, 7 pm
Sept. 1	DT Outreach service in the main sanctuary, 6 pm, for the whole congregation. P. Shannon
Sept. 2	DT Outreach service Sunday morning. PM, "Hero High" Matinee 3:30 pm, "Hero High" Evening Program 7 pm
Sept. 7	"Hero High" Dayton Public School?

SAMPLE PARENT VOLUNTEER SIGN-UP FORM FOR OUTREACHES AND EVENTS

VOLUNTEER COMMITTEE SELECTION FORM

The success of each Hope Church event depends on our volunteers! We encourage each parent to serve on at least one committee. Please choose one or more areas of interest from the following list. Thank you for your help.

Please check which committee(s) you are able to do.

☐ **Cast Party:** Help organize, plan, and execute cast party.

☐ **Costume Coordinator:** Thrift store shopping, altering, repairing, and fabricating costumes.

☐ **Props Coordinator:** Help gather necessary props for the show (s). Keep them neat and organized.

☐ **Set Team:** Help build/tear down set(s), paint, etc.

☐ **T-Shirt Sales:** Help sell and distribute show T-shirts.

☐ **Prayer Team:** Continually lift up the leaders and cast during rehearsals, throughout the week, and during the performances

☐ **Make-Up/Hair:** Assist the cast in timely getting their make-up, hair, andcostumes on.

☐ **Hospitality Team:** Assist/greet guests as they come in, as well as helping with door prizes, sign-ups, and being available for questions during the performances.

☐ **Food Coordinator:** Organize food/decorations for cast party, tech nights, and performances.

Note: any purchases must be approved and a purchase order completed by our Hope Kids Staff.

Please print the following information:

Parent Name(s): _____

Parent Cell Number: (___) _____ Home Phone: (___) _____

Cast Member's Name(s): _____

E-mail: _____

AFTER ACTION REPORT

Event   Date:

Name: Area of Responsibility:

What really helped you in preparing for the event?

What changes do you think would help for next year?

What worked well?

What didn't work well?

What, if any, changes would be needed to the budget in your area?

Any other ideas or comments for us.

Thank you for your time. We appreciate you!

ABOUT THE AUTHOR

Pastor Trisha Peach

For over 17 years, Pastor Trisha has been partnering with kids and families to create cutting edge kids' and family ministries. Her motto is: Nothing matters more than reaching this next generation for Jesus, so let's make an impact that will last! Pastor Trisha shares her life and ministry with her husband, Scott, and their two young children, Logan and Eliana. Pastor Trish is an ordained minister with a passion to empower and encourage other children's ministers in their efforts to reach these precious kids and families for Jesus.

Connect with Pastor Trisha today:
pastortrisha@gmail.com
twitter.com/Ptrishapeach
facebook.com/pastortrisha

MEET THE ILLUSTRATOR: MATT CORFITS

When Matt is not illustrating books, he loves spending time with his wife and three kids, hunting with family in Minnesota, and serving in student ministries.

TINA HOUSER, BOOK EDITOR
NICOLE IRONS, LAYOUT DESIGNER

39133618R00068

Made in the USA
Lexington, KY
15 May 2019